TWISTS OF FAITH

Ministry With Youth
at the
Turning Points of Their Lives

Marcey Balcomb and Kevin Witt

DISCIPLESHIP RESOURCES

P.O. BOX 840 • NASHVILLE, TENNESSEE 37202-0840

www.discipleshipresources.org

Cover and book design by Sharon Anderson

Library of Congress Card Catalog No. 98-96832

ISBN 0-88177-251-8

DR251

CONTENTS

INTRODUCTION

ow do youth know that God is with us? Through experience. Over the years, we've noticed a pattern: Young people frequently develop a deep awareness of God in the midst of what's happening in their own lives. Learning concepts about God hardly compares to experiencing God. It's like the difference between looking at a picture of the Rocky Mountains and actually being there, hiking in the Rockies.

We offer this book to encourage you to "be there" with youth. Walk with them in the midst of the twists and turns, the changes and discoveries, of their lives. You will find opportunities there that no classroom or program can ever provide. God is already there. *Your* profound role is to help youth reflect on their experiences in the light of God—to seek, to recognize, and to share an embrace with God.

Youth need adults who point in the direction of *hope*. Transitions and changes are often confusing and sometimes downright painful. So often youth feel like victims of fate. They feel that forces beyond their control are determining their future. If you stay in tune with what's happening in their lives, you can bring some good news to difficult situations, assuring them: "God is with you and for you. You may not have chosen this situation, but as a child of God you can choose how you will respond." A twist of *fate* can be transformed into a twist of *faith*—hence the title of this book.

Opportunities to help youth grow in their faith will definitely occur for all adults who truly care for and spend time with youth. As an adult, you only need to be alert and flexible, because normally you do not get to schedule when these defining moments arise. You do not have to be a professional youth minister, pastor, or trainer. In fact, this book is written for a wide range of adults who care about youth. You may be a volunteer, a parent or grandparent, an extended family member, a counselor, a teacher, a coach, a friend, a camp/retreat leader, a church member, or a neighbor. All of you can make a critical difference by helping young people in your family or community connect with God, who loves them. Think about this. As a

5

person of faith, if you don't encourage the youth you know to seek God, who will? You can do it!

We wrote this book to help you. The first section explores why transition times are so powerful in shaping the lives of youth. It offers ways for you to prepare yourself to be a spiritual leader whom young people trust. We examine how Jesus invites people to action and/or reflection in their lives as a way to guide them to a stronger faith. In all of this, you are not alone; support is available from many sources.

The second section of the book examines eight specific types of turning points common among youth. We share strategies about how each of these turning points might become a "twist of faith" for teenagers. Suggested sample activities are incorporated to spark your imagination and to get youth focused on each turning point. The introduction to Section Two describes in more detail how these latter chapters are designed.

TWISTS OF FAITH is different from most other youth-ministry resources, because it is not a set program or curriculum. Instead, it endeavors to teach a type of awareness and a set of skills that apply to many situations. We want you to expand on what you read and to be creative, for this book only cracks the door open to a host of other possibilities.

In faith, hope, and love,
Marcey and Kevin

SECTION ONE

THE POWER OF TURNING POINTS

The phrase *turning point* refers to a time in someone's life when decisive change takes place. These experiences significantly shape a person's life. Most of these defining moments, whether dramatic or gradual, develop during the discomfort or excitement of newness. Even an ordinary experience seen in a fresh way can produce a change that sets a new direction. The choices people make and how they understand themselves often directly connect to turning-point experiences. What happens has an effect, but how people reflect on and interpret what happens affects them far more.

What transforms a turning point into a twist of faith? What do turning points have to do with Christian youth ministry? How would you describe the unique focus of Christian youth ministry? What makes it distinct from other youth activities and organizations? These are not rhetorical questions. A well-considered response gives the direction and focus that characterize highly effective ministries with young people. Perhaps such a response has seemed so obvious that you have never thought about it deeply.

THE MISSION OF CHRISTIAN YOUTH MINISTRY IS . . .

_____

_____

_____

Take time right now to formulate a sentence that expresses your current understanding of the central mission of Christian youth ministry.

To invite youth to begin the Christian journey, we leaders need to know clearly what path we want them to explore. It's easy to get sidetracked by thinking that our primary role is to provide fun, safe activities for young people. Many organizations offer fun, safe activities. We can busily plan and lead a plethora of experiences and still fail to fulfill our unique mission. Activities serve as important tools and methods that can aid us; but they are not, in and of themselves, the purpose of Christian youth ministry. What, then, are we trying to accomplish?

In preparing to write this book, we spent huge amounts of time exploring the answer to this question with many Christian adults who actively support youth. Time after time, the conversation generated long lists of worthy goals, such as creating a caring place to belong, learning leadership skills, providing recreation, sponsoring service opportunities, and taking retreats into the natural environment.

No one would deny the benefits of these endeavors. However, when asked to identify the single most essential, enduring reason for engaging and leading youth, people responded with remarkable agreement: Our role is to help young people enter into a deeper relationship with God and embrace a Christlike way of being. If communities or people of faith fail to do this, who will? It's vitally important to cherish the deep meaning and beauty of this calling.

Few Christian adults would deliberately ignore leading the youth they love into a deeper faith experience. They may, however, inadvertently busy themselves—and thus consume their energy and focus—in ways that only marginally express the spiritual life. Instead, adults should endeavor to make activities, programs, and daily practices thoughtful avenues to a richer relationship with God. We will never consistently engage our youth in spiritual growth unless we remain ever mindful of who we are and what we are about.

Most of us know that variety and fun draw and retain youth, which is crucial if we are to gain their attention. Unfortunately, we can interest and involve youth, and still never help them grow closer to God and live as people of faith. We need fewer activity directors and program planners and more spiritual mentors!

Some of the greatest opportunities we have for making an impact on youth and for helping them recognize God's presence come during unexpected times and situations—turning points. These opportunities grow out of what happens in the lives of the youth themselves. Such moments typically involve a significant change, or the prospect of change, that a teenager faces. Some turning points might be disconcerting or quite joyful. Other turning points may seem small and insignificant; however, a series of minor changes can combine to produce major shifts.

It is vital for those of us involved in ministries of faith-formation to realize the potential inherent in transition times. Various fields of study offer insights into the richness connected with change. Biology offers the concept of *transition zones*. These zones are areas where two distinct ecosystems merge and overlap, providing greater capacity for diversity in plant and animal life. In a similar way, human beings experience increased possibilities for their lives as they move from one situation to another. Ever-present among these possibilities is a movement toward a deeper faith and relationship with God. A spiritual leader working in concert with the Holy Spirit serves as a catalyst for spiritual growth in transition zones.

Psychology points out the link between *emotion* and powerful *memories.* The memories that we recall most readily normally tie to experiences that evoke strong feelings. They may be moments that elicit fear, gratitude, suffering, celebration, peace, a sense of belonging, and so forth. Significant turning points for an individual frequently involve these types of emotions and memories. The most important concept to understand is that powerful memories continue to influence and to shape us over time. Imagine the difference it would make if youth sensed the love and grace of God as part of the memory that continues to influence them, perhaps for a lifetime. Turning points can become twists of faith.

Educators understand the value of *experiential learning.* Profound insights often occur through reflection on actual life experiences. This is particularly true for children and youth who learn more readily by doing—active learning. Young people are much more interested in learning about a subject when it clearly seems relevant to other dimensions of their lives. For example, a young person is much more interested in contemplating what happens beyond death if someone close to them has recently died or is seriously ill. Death and new life move from distant, vague ideas to personal issues.

What if a young person had an adult in his or her life who cared enough to be aware of what the youth was going through, and who was aware of her or his personal interests? What would it mean to have a parent, camp counselor, youth worker, or friend in the faith with the flexibility and willingness to offer support? What would it mean to have a trusted adult present and involved to help explore spiritual truths at the moment when these are especially applicable? The twists and turns of life often create a greater openness to being a learner—a disciple. If we miss these moments, we surely overlook unmatched opportunities to nurture Christian faith.

You may still wonder: *What's the big deal? A lot of teenagers go through change without the benefit of faith, and most survive. Do we, as Christians, have anything substantial to offer young people?* The answer is an unequivocal yes! That is the reason for this book.

Christians have a profound message that all young people long for, a message that shapes the way they understand themselves. No matter where young people go, or what they do or experience, God loves them. They are not alone. God's presence remains trustworthy; they can stake their lives on it. We should never assume that teenagers know that God is ever faithful, especially during disorienting shifts that characterize the journeys of almost everyone at this age. The following real-life stories illustrate this point.

A Story of Faith

When I was a teenager, I had an experience that continues to shape me even today. I left home to pursue an educational opportunity. Even though I received lots of accolades as a student, the separation from close friends and family left me feeling utterly alone. No one in this new place really knew me, or seemed very eager to get to know me. Back home people loved having me around. This whole educational adventure struck me as a terrible mistake.

One evening when I was particularly distraught, I took a walk to try to "pray it out." God seemed nowhere to be found. I felt like I was talking to myself. *Forget all this,* I thought. *I'm out of here!* As I turned to retrace my steps, my eyes scanned the horizon, and the scene blew me away.

Millions of stars flickered crystal clear against the jet black of night. The beauty nearly brought me to tears. A wave of peace passed through me, and suddenly I knew God was with me. I sensed without a doubt that I was not alone and that things would be all right. This assurance came from beyond myself. It filled me. I shouted at the top of my voice into the great expanse, "Thank you, God!" The praise came so spontaneously, so naturally.

For the first time, the words from the Book of Hebrews began to make sense. "Now faith is the assurance of things hoped for, the conviction of things not seen. . . . By faith we understand that the worlds were prepared by the word of God, so that what is seen was made from things that are not visible" (Hebrews 11:1, 3). I felt God at the core of the universe and at the core of my own being. I cannot overstate how much it has meant throughout my life to realize that there is a Presence with me and for me—a Presence behind and within every person, every creature. Even though God, the Creator, is unseen, God is very real. This assurance—this faith—makes all the difference. The very existence of the stars themselves speaks of God. Even stars are a word from God, if we have eyes to see and ears to hear.

In retrospect, now that I am an adult, it seems entirely possible that I may have been completely oblivious to one of the most defining moments of my life. I could have missed it altogether. If important adults had not encouraged me to seek God when I was a youth, would I have been able to perceive the connection between beauty and its Creator? If no one had helped me learn to pray, would I have even taken the walk to pray it out? If my Sunday school teachers, camp counselors, youth sponsors, parents, and others never introduced me to the Scriptures, would the passage from Hebrews have been in my frame of reference to add deeper meaning to that experience? I seriously doubt it.

Even though the caring adults who helped shape my faith were not physically present when that turning point in my life occurred, through their preparation, love, and teaching, they walked with me. I suspect these mentors never fully understood the profound impact their spiritual leadership had, and continues to have, in enriching my faith and my existence.

Never underestimate the difference you can make. If you are reading this book, you care about youth and their relationship with God. Continue on! Often it seems like nothing dramatic is happening in our ministry with youth, but don't be fooled. Connections with God take root under the surface, then bear fruit when the time is right. Have faith. God moves among us.

A Story of Hope

I answered the phone one morning. A woman's voice, which I did not recognize, immediately launched into an explanation of the reason for her call. Lisa, a student in my youth group, had specifically named me as a support person in her life. The woman on the line was the high school counselor. I sat stunned as she informed me that Lisa's father had died—it was sudden and unexpected.

As I hung up the phone, my mind rushed with thoughts about the implications of this tragedy. I knew Lisa's father, so lots of feelings churned inside me for Lisa and for her family. It was hard to grasp what would be most helpful in this situation. Minutes later, the phone rang again. It was Lisa's mother. She was not active in a faith community, and our previous contact, though gracious, was very limited. Her despair made it difficult for her to even speak. "Will you come over to our house right away? We need you. Lisa said that I should call you. I can't handle this alone. Please?"

While driving to Lisa's house I wrestled in my heart with feelings of inadequacy. How in the world could I help? I was being invited into their private space at an extremely personal time. I nearly panicked at the thought of how unprepared and ill-equipped I felt in relation to what might be asked of me.

My prayers grew more intense as I neared the home. "Why me, God? Surely someone else could handle this better than me!" And yet, in the midst of the storm, this family called *me*. They sought someone connected with God, someone they trusted. Lisa had learned the stories of Jesus through her years in the youth group, and now she was turning to the One who calmed the storm (Matthew 8:23-27). Now was my opportunity to encourage this family to lean on God. I continued to pray, "God, help them. Help me help them. Please be there."

When I arrived, Lisa came running out the door, sobbing uncontrollably in her grief. She wrapped her arms tightly around me and held on as if she would never let go. That's when I realized that all I really needed to do was simply be present. I promised to stay with them for a while. They wanted to be reassured of God's love for them and for the father and husband whose loss they mourned. They needed a tangible expression of the life that never ends—a person to confirm their hope in new beginnings as they started to deal with a tragic ending. Hope!

The day seemed to last forever, and the night even longer. God's loving arms embraced us as we held on tightly to one another, awaiting a new dawn. Lisa and her mom longed for an affirmation of God's loving presence. Psalm 46 expresses it so well.

> God is our refuge and strength,
>   a very present help in trouble.
> Therefore we will not fear,
>   though the earth should change,
>   though the mountains shake in the heart of the sea;
> though its waters roar and foam,
>   though the mountains tremble with its tumult.
>
> (Psalm 46:1-3)

I learned that hope exists so powerfully that it sustains people at the most chaotic crossroads of their lives. The apostle Paul describes this assurance by saying, "I can do all things through [Christ] who strengthens me" (Philippians 4:13). This kind of hope emerges from a fundamental trust that God exists and loves us. Herein lies the purpose of being a caring Christian adult in ministry with teenagers: to help youth recognize and experience God, and then to support them as they develop a faith of their own founded on love. There is nothing more important for us to do.

A Story of Love

Carmen was angry with herself and her situation, and she had good reasons. The struggles she had been through had hardened her at an early age. She raised shields of aloofness and sarcasm to protect herself from difficult external circumstances. However, these defenses could not protect her from the turmoil and doubt growing within her about her own worth and place in the world. Those closest to her worried about her future and the choices she would make. Carmen had so much going for her, but she sometimes seemed completely unaware of her own strengths and gifts. Where would this lead? What paths would she take? Would she even survive? The uncertainty was frightening.

Someone she respected invited her to participate in a church youth group. Let's just say she resisted. It took a great deal of gentle persuasion before she agreed to start attending regularly. Others in the group found her difficult to relate with. She often simply refused to respond when someone tried to talk with her. She intimidated both the youth and many adults by her steady gaze that defied any attempt to get close. One day she seemed finally to engage with people, only to lash out or withdraw the very next day. She continued to be as unpredictable as the emotions whirling inside her. Folks realized early on that it was naive to expect quick solutions to the dilemma.

Fortunately this particular group of youth and adults resolved to love her and to accept her despite the hassles. "Love is patient; love is kind; love is not envious or boastful or arrogant or rude. It does not insist on its own way; it is not irritable or resentful; it does not rejoice in wrongdoing, but rejoices in the truth. It bears all things, believes all things, hopes all things, endures all things. Love never ends" (1 Corinthians 13:4-8a). Love never fails, but sometimes people falter. It was not easy to live out such love; nor was it easy for the young woman to receive it at first.

This community of adults and youth enacted over and over again the characteristics of love found in 1 Corinthians 13. Despite imperfection, they were consistent in their care and concern. Over a number of years, a transformation took place. Carmen became a capable leader within the group. Her confidence increased. She grew to be a loving, caring person herself. Others began to learn from her.

Now it's sometimes hard to think back and fathom that this individual is the same person who first entered the group. In truth, Carmen is not the same person. She is clearly different now. Love is powerful.

Who can say where she might have ended up? She now knows that she is valued. She possesses a greater capacity to make a difference. In pursuing a new way of being, she discovered a more abundant life. She cooperates with God in her own healing, and her faith is making her well. Perhaps her story does not seem remarkable because there are many similar stories—but it is no less a miracle. In some ways, we know that her story speaks to our own stories.

Let's Reclaim the Heart of Ministry With Youth

One goal of this book is to inspire adults who care about youth to lead these young people to what really lasts. And what *does* really last? What remains when everything else fades away? What can a person base his or her life on? The themes of the three stories on the previous pages illustrate what is at the very heart of youth ministry: *faith, hope,* and *love.* More than anything else, youth need these to find fulfillment in their lives.

In 1 Corinthians 13 Paul talks about the hollowness of even the greatest of human accomplishments and gifts if these are not founded on and infused with love. He talks about how, in the end, much of what we value will pass away, including what we think we know. "And now faith, hope, and love abide, these three; and the greatest of these is love" (1 Corinthians 13:13).

When we talk about the primary purpose of youth ministry being faith formation and discipleship, we mean leading youth to become people who actively seek God and who live from a center of faith, hope, and love. What can we possibly do that would be of greater lasting value for our own children and for the youth of our communities? Everything else fades and does not last.

WHAT IS FAITH?

Faith is the deep trust that God is with us and for us.

WHAT IS HOPE?

Hope is the expectation and belief that we will receive what is truly needed, even though it is not yet fully apparent in a situation.

WHAT IS LOVE?

Love is God cherishing all of creation, and it is humanity's response to that care. Love is choosing to make the effort to nourish growth in God for yourself and others.

As Christians, we have a unique perspective to bring to the meaning of faith, hope, and love. It is the great joy and privilege of Christians to share one of the most profound ways that God has ever been revealed: Jesus Christ. Here is the treasure given to the Christian church to take to the world, in word and in action. Jesus Christ is called "Emmanuel," which means "God is with us." (See Matthew 1:23.) An important part of what Christian adults do for youth is introducing them to Jesus Christ and to "the Way" that he taught and lived. We should not shy away from this.

We address these words to all Christians, whether liberal, conservative, or somewhere in between. All of us should cherish our identity as Christians and should cherish the path that Jesus has shown. What remains to be given if we fail to celebrate the good news of our faith? We have been shown one of the most enduring paths to God. It would be no less than a tragedy for everyone, especially for the youth in our midst, if we fail to appreciate and to celebrate our Christian heritage, along with the continually growing understanding of what it means to be a Christian in a changing world.

Sharing Christ in a Changing World

It may seem strange that we would even mention the importance of sharing the Christian path to God. Many people make the assumption that this is so obvious that it need not be lifted up. American society, however, continues to undergo fundamental changes that have an impact on this very issue. God is doing a new thing, and some of us, as Christian leaders, struggle to know how to respond.

American society today is becoming increasingly diverse and pluralistic, and this is contributing to the confusion and hesitancy that many Christians feel about their faith. Tremendous strides have been taken toward creating a deep respect for and an appreciation of differences. This includes becoming more aware that faith traditions beyond the Christian church can offer insights into the nature of God. This mutual learning is truly good. Some spiritual practices and reflections from other religions remind us of lost or overlooked aspects of our own Christian teachings and traditions. We must reclaim these lost traditions in new ways if we are to thrive in these new times and new circumstances. It takes us beyond the tunnel vision that can be so limiting and so destructive to any faith tradition.

Unfortunately, many Christians have not understood what is at the heart of this new spiritual dialogue. We equate honoring other faiths with passive rejection of our own Christian spiritual traditions. The dialogue between faiths is intended to strengthen our connection with God, not weaken it. It is not a call to abandon or to hide our faith, but rather to live it more fully and more compassionately.

Instead of broadening the depth of what it means to be Christian, many of us now feel awkward and unsure about being followers of Christ at all. In so doing we completely miss the point and withhold the particular message God has given us to enrich the world. It is crucial to consciously recognize this hesitancy, for it affects our family practices, our willingness or desire to invite new people into our local communities of faith (including youth), the willingness or desire on the part of camp and retreat centers to identify with the church and spiritual growth, and our willingness or desire to make faith formation the focus of our ministries. Ultimately, it means that some youth will not be led toward the faith, hope, and love that is so essential to life, because we do not fully embrace our own Christian identity and path.

This kind of thinking also creates havoc in the minds of youth, who learn from watching important adults in their lives. When we seem bored or embarrassed by being Christian, it teaches our youth to feel the same, even if we do not intend to pass those feelings along. If all the adherents of every faith thought like this, who would ever guide people to a deeper connection with God?

Christians during the time of the apostle Paul also expressed uncertainty about their faith. As a Christian leader, Paul shared these words with the church in Rome: "I am not ashamed of the gospel; it is the power of God for salvation to everyone who has faith, to the Jew first and also to the Greek. For in it the righteousness of God is revealed through faith for faith; as it is written, 'The one who is righteous will live by faith' " (Romans 1:16-17). Christ as a revelation and an avenue to God has not changed.

May we as Christian leaders learn to honor God by cherishing the Christian path and by inviting others—especially youth—to join us on the journey. Society rightly reminds us of times in history when we Christians have not lived the love we profess. Such a reminder is not intended as a dismissal of the Christian path; rather, it is an expression of anger and dismay that Christians have, at times, failed to live the way of love they profess. We also live in a time when nearly everything in our culture is being doubted. Negativity and skepticism reign. It would be easy for us Christians to allow ourselves to be completely defined by these voices and by our own insecurities. That is why we need to remember that it is God who defines us, not our culture!

It's time for many of us, as adult Christians in this society, to choose a turning point in our own faith and perspective. Despite our failures Christ continues to reveal God to us, and the Christian path continues to represent a profound way to God. The Holy Spirit continues to bring love to the world through the church in every place where we truly live as the body of Christ. Lives are transformed. It's so important to help people engage in this work of God, especially young people who are forming lifelong understandings through their experiences.

On to Faith, Hope, and Love!

Are we going to leave the spiritual growth of young people purely to chance? As a Christian leader in ministry with youth, or as a Christian adult who cares about youth, it is essential to introduce young people to the wonder of "God is with us" in Jesus Christ. If Christians don't do this, who will? Young people long to see in us the passion, the joy, the thought, and the action that arise when we believe in God. Our active faith in Christ, who speaks the word of love in a million ways, encourages their faith.

In the beginning was the Word, and the Word was with God, and the Word was God. . . . All things came into being through him, and without him not one thing came into being. . . . [I]n him was life, and the life was the light of all people. The light shines in the darkness, and the darkness did not overcome it . . . And the Word became flesh and lived among us, and we have seen his glory.

(John 1:1, 3-5, 14a)

CHAPTER 2

SACRED AWARENESS

J esus spent his ministry helping people become aware of, and experience, the Sacred. It's fascinating to read the Gospels to observe how Jesus did this. He constantly invited people to action and/or reflection based upon the hopeful, loving presence of God. In a real way, youth ministry continues this process of learning to live on the basis of the presence of God. Faith takes shape in the midst of the experiences of life. Jesus was a master at making the most of teachable moments. The Bible provides many accounts of how Jesus led and taught people. We encourage you to study and to incorporate his approaches in order to strengthen your own leadership.

In preparing to write this chapter, we read all four Gospels from beginning to end. This was time well spent, because in reading all four Gospels at one time, patterns began to emerge that would have remained unnoticed had we read only single passages. Based on our reading, we selected from Jesus' ministry a number of key aspects that made it so effective. Observing the ways in which Jesus intentionally guided people to a deeper faith provides insight for our ministry with youth. In what follows, watch how he guided people toward faith, hope, and love.

Jesus Clarified His Purpose

As a spiritual leader, Jesus was very clear about his purpose. Both his words and his actions reflected that primary aim in a variety of ways. It's critically important for us to concretely define our primary purpose as spiritual leaders among young people. In order to be effective, we must clearly know what we are trying to accomplish.

- . . . Jesus came to Galilee, proclaiming the good news of God. (Mark 1:14)

- When he came to Nazareth, where he had been brought up, he went to the synagogue on the sabbath day, as was his custom. He stood up to read, and the scroll of the prophet Isaiah was given to him. He unrolled the scroll and found the place where it was written:

"The Spirit of the Lord is upon me,
  because he has anointed me to bring good news to the poor.
He has sent me to proclaim release to the captives
  and recovery of sight to the blind,
    to let the oppressed go free,
to proclaim the year of the Lord's favor."

And he rolled up the scroll, gave it back to the attendant, and sat down. The eyes of all in the synagogue were fixed on him. Then he began to say to them, "Today this scripture has been fulfilled in your hearing." (Luke 4:16-21)

• Indeed, God did not send the Son into the world to condemn the world, but in order that the world might be saved through him.
(John 3:17)

Jesus Was Among the People

Jesus was out there among the people, there where they lived their lives. He encountered an amazing diversity of individuals, from community leaders to those on the fringes of society. Jesus surprised a lot of people by whom he talked, ate, and associated with in his endeavor to connect people with God.

• A Samaritan woman came to draw water, and Jesus said to her, "Give me a drink." (His disciples had gone to the city to buy food.) The Samaritan woman said to him, "How is it that you, a Jew, ask a drink of me, a woman of Samaria?" (Jews do not share things in common with Samaritans.) . . . Just then his disciples came. They were astonished that he was speaking with a woman, but no one said, "What do you want?" or, "Why are you speaking with her?" Then the woman left her water jar and went back to the city. She said to the people, "Come and see a man who told me everything I have ever done! He cannot be the Messiah, can he?" . . . Many Samaritans from that city believed in him because of the woman's testimony. . . . So when the Samaritans came to him, they asked him to stay with them; and he stayed there two days. And many more believed because of his word.
(John 4:7-9, 27-29, 39-41)

• A man was there named Zacchaeus; he was a chief tax collector and was rich. He was trying to see who Jesus was, but on account of the crowd he could not, because he was short in stature. So he ran ahead and climbed a sycamore tree to see him, because he was going to pass that way. When Jesus came to the place, he looked up and said to him, "Zacchaeus, hurry and come down; for I must stay at your house today." So he hurried down and was happy to welcome him. All who saw it began to grumble and said, "He has gone to be the guest of one who is a sinner." Zacchaeus stood there and said to the Lord, "Look, half of my possessions, Lord, I will give to the poor; and if I have defrauded anyone of anything, I will pay back four times as much." Then Jesus said to him, "Today salvation has come to this house, because he too is a son of Abraham. For the Son of Man came to seek out and to save the lost."   (Luke 19:2-10)

Jesus Participated in Healing

Jesus spent time with those who were suffering; he did not avoid these people. Jesus frequently asked people who were suffering to participate in their own healing, or he helped them recognize that they had participated. We may not possess the gifts for healing in the same way that Jesus did, but we can definitely bring hope and life in the midst of difficult situations. Adult leaders participate in healing by encouraging youth to lean on God in faith. Our presence with them is part of God's loving presence. These simple acts can lead to amazing results.

- When he entered Capernaum, a centurion came to him, appealing to him and saying, "Lord, my servant is lying at home paralyzed, in terrible distress." And he said to him, "I will come and cure him." The centurion answered, "Lord, I am not worthy to have you come under my roof; but only speak the word, and my servant will be healed. For I also am a man under authority, with soldiers under me; and I say to one, 'Go,' and he goes, and to another, 'Come,' and he comes, and to my slave, 'Do this,' and the slave does it." When Jesus heard him, he was amazed and said to those who followed him, "Truly I tell you, in no one in Israel have I found such faith."   (Matthew 8:5-10)

- Again he entered the synagogue, and a man was there who had a withered hand. They watched him to see whether he would cure him on the sabbath, so that they might accuse him. And he said to the man who had the withered hand, "Come forward." Then he said to them, "Is it lawful to do good or to do harm on the sabbath, to save life or to kill?" But they were silent. He looked around at them with anger; he was grieved at their hardness of heart and said to the man, "Stretch out your hand." He stretched it out, and his hand was restored.   (Mark 3:1-5)

Jesus Invited People to Follow

Jesus called people to become part of a group who shared experiences with him. They spent time together, journeyed to new places, and did things they had never done before. Jesus used these journeys to teach them the way of God. He claimed his role as a teacher. Youth leaders and youth can embark on journeys of various kinds and follow Jesus, even today. A couple of prime examples related to youth ministry would be mission trips or outings to places the youth have never been.

• As he walked by the Sea of Galilee, he saw two brothers, Simon, who is called Peter, and Andrew his brother, casting a net into the sea—for they were fishermen. And he said to them, "Follow me, and I will make you fish for people." Immediately they left their nets and followed him. As he went from there, he saw two other brothers, James son of Zebedee and his brother John, in the boat with their father Zebedee, mending their nets, and he called them. Immediately they left the boat and their father, and followed him.   (Matthew 4:18-22)

• Whoever serves me must follow me, and where I am, there will my servant be also. Whoever serves me, the Father will honor.

(John 12:26)

Jesus Used Parables, Stories, Metaphors, and Real-Life Examples

Jesus inspired people to reflect more deeply on and to develop new understandings of a spiritual truth by comparing that truth to something they already knew. He used familiar plants, fictitious stories about people's lives, everyday activities, and more to bring spiritual insight. Often Jesus did not explain the meaning of the spiritual truth immediately, leaving people to consider for themselves what it might mean. This strategy reminds people of the truth, even when the teacher is not present.

What things that our youth are familiar with today might become illustrations of spiritual truth? For example, the Kingdom of God is like jet travel. It takes you places you've never been before; and even if you return, you are never the same. Youth could spend hours discussing the meaning of such metaphors or creating their own.

• And again he said, "To what should I compare the kingdom of God? It is like yeast that a woman took and mixed in with three measures of flour until all of it was leavened."   (Luke 13:20-21)

• I am the vine, you are the branches. Those who abide in me and I in them bear much fruit, because apart from me you can do nothing.

(John 15:5)

• Then Jesus told them a parable about their need to pray always and not to lose heart. He said, "In a certain city there was a judge who neither feared God nor had respect for people. In that city there was a widow who kept coming to him and saying, 'Grant me justice against my opponent.' For a while he refused; but later he said to himself, 'Though I have no fear of God and no respect for anyone, yet because this widow keeps bothering me, I will grant her justice, so that she may not wear me out by continually coming.'" And the Lord said, "Listen to what the unjust judge says. And will not God grant justice to his chosen ones who cry to him day and night? Will he delay long in helping them? I tell you, he will quickly grant justice to them. And yet, when the Son of Man comes, will he find faith on earth?"   (Luke 18:1-8)

Jesus Used Questions . . . and More Questions

Jesus habitually used questions as a forum for teaching and guiding. He responded to genuine questions from those who were truly seeking. Sometimes Jesus chose to respond to a question with another question so people might delve deeper into the truth. He asked questions of his own. Often Jesus refused to respond directly to people who argued for the sake of arguing or who tried to manipulate him, because they were not truly interested in learning. Anytime a youth asks you an important question, the potential for spiritual growth is high. Sometimes a youth is looking for a direct response, while at other times it is an invitation to explore the meaning of his or her life in one way or another. Sometimes the best answer is another question for the teenager to consider.

- Then Peter came and said to him, "Lord, if another member of the church sins against me, how often should I forgive? As many as seven times?" Jesus said to him, "Not seven times, but, I tell you, seventy-seven times."   (Matthew 18:21-22)

- When he saw their faith, he said, "Friend, your sins are forgiven you." Then the scribes and the Pharisees began to question, "Who is this who is speaking blasphemies? Who can forgive sins but God alone?" When Jesus perceived their questionings, he answered them, "Why do you raise such questions in your hearts? Which is easier, to say, 'Your sins are forgiven you,' or to say, 'Stand up and walk'?"   (Luke 5:20-23)

- When they had finished breakfast, Jesus said to Simon Peter, "Simon son of John, do you love me more than these?" He said to him, "Yes, Lord; you know that I love you." Jesus said to him, "Feed my lambs." A second time he said to him, "Simon son of John, do you love me?" He said to him, "Yes, Lord; you know that I love you." Jesus said to him, "Tend my sheep." He said to him the third time, "Simon son of John, do you love me?" Peter felt hurt because he said to him the third time, "Do you love me?" And he said to him, "Lord, you know everything; you know that I love you." Jesus said to him, "Feed my sheep."   (John 21:15-17)

Jesus Prayed Often

Because Jesus prayed regularly, Jesus' followers knew that God was real and important to him. Jesus did not pray to be noticed; he prayed as a way of being with God. Prayer was a regular part of Jesus' life, enriching his faith in God. When people observed that, their faith was enriched also. What is more, Jesus taught his disciples how to pray and assured them that God cared about them and heard their petitions. It may seem simplistic, and yet youth notice that God is important to you because you regularly communicate with God. We need to introduce youth to the many forms of prayer.

- But now more than ever the word about Jesus spread abroad; many crowds would gather to hear him and to be cured of their diseases. But he would withdraw to deserted places and pray.   (Luke 5:15-16)

- They went to a place called Gethsemane; and he said to his disciples, "Sit here while I pray." He took with him Peter and James and John, and began to be distressed and agitated. And said to them, "I am deeply grieved, even to death; remain here, and keep awake." And going a little farther, he threw himself on the ground and prayed that, it were possible, the hour might pass from him.   (Mark 14:32-35)

- When you are praying, do not heap up empty phrases as the Gentiles do; for they think that they will be heard because of their many words. Do not be like them, for your Father knows what you need before you ask him.   (Matthew 6:7-8)

Jesus Knew Scripture and the Tradition

Jesus studied and was familiar with the Scriptures, as well as with religious teaching. He reminded people of passages that had meaning in the current situation. Often he applied Scripture and tradition in unexpected ways to emphasize what was truly important, in contrast to what was peripheral. His use of biblical passages and sayings was poignant because he chose carefully the opportunities to apply these rather than reciting Scripture *ad nauseam*. It is important for us as leaders to study and be familiar with the Scriptures so that we can effectively connect real-life experiences with biblical insights.

- In everything do to others as you would have them do to you; for this is the law and the prophets.   (Matthew 7:12)

- One of the scribes came near and heard them disputing with one another, and seeing that he answered them well, he asked him, "Which commandment is the first of all?" Jesus answered, "The first is, 'Hear, O Israel: the Lord our God, the Lord is one; you shall love the Lord your God with all your heart, and with all your soul, and with all your mind, and with all your strength.' The second is this, 'You shall love your neighbor as yourself.' There is no other commandment greater than these." Then the scribe said to him, "You are right, Teacher; you have truly said that 'he is one, and besides him there is no other'; and 'to love him with all the heart, and with all the understanding, and with all the strength', and 'to love one's neighbor as oneself,'—this is much more important than all whole burnt offerings and sacrifices." When Jesus saw that he answered wisely, he said to him, "You are not far from the kingdom of God." After that no one dared to ask him any question.   (Mark 12:28-34)

- Then Pharisees and scribes came to Jesus from Jerusalem and said, "Why do your disciples break the tradition of the elders? For they do not wash their hands before they eat." He answered them, "And why do you break the commandment of God for the sake of your tradition? For God said, 'Honor your father and your mother,' and, 'Whoever speaks evil of father or mother must surely die.' But you say that whoever tells father or mother, 'Whatever support you might have had from me is given to God,' then that person need not honor the father. So, for the sake of your tradition, you make void the word of God. You hypocrites! Isaiah prophesied rightly about you when he said:

  'This people honors me with their lips,
      but their hearts are far from me;
  in vain do they worship me,
      teaching human precepts as doctrines.'"

                                                                                                    (Matthew 15:1-9)

Jesus Practiced Empathy and Forgiveness

Jesus tended to be much more forgiving and empathetic than many of the people of his time. He regularly embraced those who were outcasts and who were rejected by society, to the consternation of some religious and community leaders. He taught his followers to care and to forgive as a matter of faith. How might empathy and forgiveness enhance your mentoring of youth?

- The scribes and the Pharisees brought a woman who had been caught in adultery; and making her stand before all of them, they said to him, "Teacher, this woman was caught in the very act of committing adultery. Now in the law Moses commanded us to stone such women. Now what do you say?" They said this to test him, so that they might have some charge to bring against him. Jesus bent down and wrote with his finger on the ground. When they kept on questioning him, he straightened up and said to them, "Let anyone among you who is without sin be the first to throw a stone at her." And once again he bent down and wrote on the ground. When they heard it, they went away, one by one, beginning with the elders; and Jesus was left alone with the woman standing before him. Jesus straightened up and said to her, "Woman, where are they? Has no one condemned you?" She said, "No one, sir." And Jesus said, "Neither do I condemn you. Go your way, and from now on do not sin again."   (John 8:3-11)

- Be merciful, just as your Father is merciful. Do not judge, and you will not be judged; do not condemn, and you will not be condemned. Forgive, and you will be forgiven; give, and it will be given to you.

(Luke 6:36-38a)

- When Mary came where Jesus was and saw him, she knelt at his feet and said to him, "Lord, if you had been here, my brother would not have died." When Jesus saw her weeping, and the Jews who came with her also weeping, he was greatly disturbed in spirit and deeply moved. He said, "Where have you laid him?" They said to him, "Lord, come and see." Jesus began to weep. So the Jews said, "See how he loved him!"

(John 11:32-36)

Jesus Provided Instructions for Living

Jesus offered his followers direct guidance to help them live by faith. He portrayed how a disciple relates with others and depends on God. He even presented the most crucial directives as commandments, because they are so important to community life. In a brilliant way, Jesus connected teachings to everyday activities so that his disciples would remember his love and guidance whenever they participated in these activities. Sometimes it is important to have the courage to give teenagers guidance instead of simply asking them what they think. Often this involves having them consider the instructions of Jesus himself.

- I give you a new commandment, that you love one another. Just as I have loved you, you also should love one another. By this everyone will know that you are my disciples, if you have love for one another.

(John 13:34-35)

- After he had washed their feet, had put on his robe, and had returned to the table, [Jesus] said to them, "Do you know what I have done to you? You call me Teacher and Lord—and you are right, for that is what I am. So if I, your Lord and Teacher, have washed your feet, you also ought to wash one another's feet. For I have set you an example, that you also should do as I have done to you. Very truly, I tell you, servants are not greater than their master, nor are messengers greater than the one who sent them. If you know these things, you are blessed if you do them."

(John 13:12-17)

- Do not judge, so that you may not be judged. For with the judgment you make you will be judged, and the measure you give will be the measure you get. Why do you see the speck in your neighbor's eye, but do not notice the log in your own eye? Or how can you say to your neighbor, "Let me take the speck out of your eye," while the log is in your own eye? You hypocrite, first take the log out of your own eye, and then you will see clearly to take the speck out of your neighbor's eye.

(Matthew 7:1-5)

- He said to his disciples, "Therefore I tell you, do not worry about your life, what you will eat, or about your body, what you will wear. For life is more than food, and the body more than clothing. Consider the ravens: they neither sow nor reap, they have neither storehouse nor barn, and yet God feeds them. Of how much more value are you than the birds! And can any of you by worrying add a single hour to your span of life?"   (Luke 12:22-25)

- Then he took a loaf of bread, and when he had given thanks, he broke it and gave it to them, saying, "This is my body, which is given for you. Do this in remembrance of me." And he did the same with the cup after supper, saying, "This cup that is poured out for you is the new covenant in my blood."   (Luke 22:19-20)

Jesus Engaged in Ministry

Jesus purposefully sent his disciples to participate in ministry for others rather than to simply observe people. Service and sacrifice characterize part of what it means to walk the Christian way. Jesus trained the disciples and then sent them out to bring life to the world—to put faith into action. After their experiences and adventures, Jesus gathered them to reflect on what had happened. Youth, in particular, learn by doing. Talking about the love of God is not nearly so powerful as acting out the love of God where it is really needed.

- Then Jesus called the twelve together and gave them power and authority over all demons and to cure diseases, and he sent them out to proclaim the kingdom of God and to heal. . . . They departed and went through the villages, bringing the good news and curing diseases everywhere. . . . On their return the apostles told Jesus all they had done. He took them with him and withdrew privately to a city called Bethsaida.   (Luke 9:1-2, 6, 10)

- As he went ashore, he saw a great crowd; and he had compassion for them, because they were like sheep without a shepherd; and he began to teach them many things. When it grew late, his disciples came to him and said, "This is a deserted place, and the hour is now very late; send them away so that they may go into the surrounding country and villages and buy something for themselves to eat." But he answered them, "You give them something to eat."

                                            (Mark 6:34-37a)

- Then the king will say to those at his right hand, "Come, you that are blessed by my Father, inherit the kingdom prepared for you from the foundation of the world; for I was hungry and you gave me food, I was thirsty and you gave me something to drink, I was a stranger and you welcomed me, I was naked and you gave me clothing, I was sick and you took care of me, I was in prison and you visited me." Then the righteous will answer him, "Lord, when was it that we saw you hungry and gave you food, or thirsty and gave you something to drink? And when was it that we saw you a stranger and welcomed you, or naked and gave you clothing? And when was it that we saw you sick or in prison and visited you?" And the king will answer them, "Truly I tell you, just as you did it to one of the least of these who are members of my family, you did it to me." (Matthew 25:34-40)

Jesus Practiced the Presence of God

Jesus reminded people that God is with them. God continues to bring life in the midst of the world. Jesus himself was a manifestation of God's presence. It is amazing how youth recognize the presence of God simply because someone reminds them to look and to listen for God in the rhythm of their everyday lives.

- Once Jesus was asked by the Pharisees when the kingdom of God was coming, and he answered, "The kingdom of God is not coming with things that can be observed; nor will they say, 'Look, here it is!' or 'There it is!' For, in fact, the kingdom of God is among you." (Luke 17:20-21)

- Look, the virgin shall conceive
     and bear a son,
   and they shall name him Emmanuel,
which means, "God is with us." (Matthew 1:23)

- In the beginning was the Word, and the Word was with God, and the Word was God. He was in the beginning with God. All things came into being through him . . . And the Word became flesh and lived among us, and we have seen his glory. (John 1:1-3, 14a)

- If you love me, you will keep my commandments. And I will ask the Father, and he will give you another Advocate [Helper], to be with you forever. This is the Spirit of truth, whom the world cannot receive, because it neither sees him nor knows him. You know him, because he abides with you, and he will be in you. I will not leave you orphaned; I am coming to you. In a little while the world will no longer see me, but you will see me; because I live, you also will live. On that day you will know that I am in my Father, and you in me, and I in you. (John 14:15-20)

Jesus and the Art of Reflection

Several common threads can be found in Jesus' approaches to helping people connect with the sacred. One of the most fascinating discoveries from studying the four Gospels is Jesus' pattern of linking spiritual reflection with actual experience. More often than not, Jesus taught and ministered in response to an occurrence or an issue that was important to people at a particular moment. For example, to a woman drawing water from a well, he taught about living water. Jesus responded to questions at the moment they were raised because he realized the need for people to have answers then and there. He participated in the healing of people who were ready to be healed. These were unplanned, teachable moments that arose out of the experiences of life. Jesus watched for these opportunities and used them as a primary method for deepening the faith of believers.

Experiences in and of themselves do not produce faith. For example, in a culture where people walk on dirt roads and pathways wearing sandals, washing feet is a common experience. How does washing feet become a powerful symbol of faith and Christian life for the first disciples, and for us? The answer is: The ordinary act of foot-washing gains new meanings—becomes a symbol of faith—through a time of reflection about the experience. Without the intentional act of reflection, a new understanding would not have occurred. Jesus deliberately initiated reflection: "Do you know what I have done to you?" (John 13:12b). Jesus could have ended the washing of his disciples' feet by simply reminding them to care for one another; however, this would not have been nearly so powerful or memorable. Deliberate reflection on action bestows important meaning.

It's interesting to note that Jesus planned the foot-washing experience. However, both planned and unplanned experiences are crucial catalysts for helping young people recognize God and the ways of God. Youth leaders miss many opportunities by failing to be attentive to the experiences of young people, or by failing to prepare themselves to reflect spiritually with the youth at the opportune times.

Thinking about religious concepts can be utterly boring if young people fail to recognize the relevance of such thinking for their lives. Even if unintentional, boredom often discourages youth from growing in their faith. When this happens, it's important to consider whether the link between reflection and experience is missing. Active learning produces active faith.

> And it happens—
> a twist of faith.

Faith formation is not always as predictable as we might like. Youth leaders must be ready to "go with the flow." They must maintain an awareness in order to recognize teachable moments and to understand when it's time to create such moments. Sometimes the youth don't seem to comprehend what their leaders are trying to convey at a particular point in time; however, during a turning point in the future, or after reflecting upon it at a later time, a young person may come to understand the point his or her leader was trying to convey.

As it is written, "The wind blows where it chooses, and you hear the sound of it, but you do not know where it comes from or where it goes. So it is with everyone who is born of the Spirit" (John 3:8). When adult leaders participate with the youth in common experiences and also stay aware of other experiences that are important to the youth, the leaders are often blessed to notice the Spirit moving in the young people's lives. And then the leaders have the privilege of helping the young people reflect on and notice a twist of faith.

THE FEAR FACTOR

egan stood six feet above the group on a stump. She trembled visibly. Those below gently encouraged her. "Don't worry, Megan. We'll catch you. No sweat. Remember Bill? He weighs 250 pounds, and we didn't drop him! You're as light as a feather. Just stay stiff and fall into our arms." Megan looked into the eyes of two rows of people facing each other with arms extended to support her. With concentration, they braced themselves to spot her properly. She began to cry.

At first a few tears fell, then Megan began sobbing uncontrollably. She stared straight ahead to avoid eye contact. The jovial mood that had permeated the morning suddenly shifted as the group perceived the tremendous internal struggle. "Megan, it's really okay not to do this. We all agreed that this challenge is by choice. Anyone can opt out of any element of the ropes course." Megan had spent a great deal of time with these people and knew they genuinely cared. She could step down, and no one would think any less of her.

Everyone waited in silent anticipation for Megan's response. She felt emotionally overwhelmed. She could not speak, but she slowly shook her head. Her hand gestured for the group to stay put until she could compose herself. She wanted to do this. For three full minutes, which seemed like an eternity, Megan stood shaking as every eye remained locked on her. It was obvious that a conversation was taking place within her as she sought the courage to take the risk. Suddenly, a glance toward those prepared to catch her signaled her intent. A moment later, she let herself go. After landing in the trustworthy arms, she hopped off so fast that it was almost comical.

Shouts of celebration echoed through the forest. Smiling, loving faces congratulated her. She stepped off to the side, contemplating what she had done in taking this "Trust Fall." Megan allowed herself the pleasure of a small smile. The remainder of the morning proceeded well as the community met one challenge after another together. At the close of their experience, they gathered to reflect on what happened. The key moment for everyone was when Megan trusted enough to fall. They began to discuss it. "It was amazing to watch Megan. That was the most special moment for me. She had a lot of courage to let herself go when she was afraid we might not catch her." Everyone nodded in complete agreement.

At this point Megan began to speak about her experience. "You don't understand. I was not afraid that you might drop me. I knew you would catch me, and that scared me terribly." This statement mystified the others. No one responded, but everyone was wondering what Megan meant by her statement.

Megan hesitated, then continued. "None of you knows this. In fact, I have not told another soul until right now. About six months ago a man molested me. I don't know who he was, but he crushed my spirit. I have not permitted any man to touch me since that day. I stood up there looking down at the arms, and fear welled up in me, because some of you are men. I did not know how to be vulnerable, even though you have done nothing but treat me kindly.

"Somehow up there on the stump, I realized that this was a turning point for me. I've got a long way to go, but today was the first step toward my healing. I cannot thank you enough for the way you have loved me. It enabled me to begin to learn how to trust again." The group sat stunned by the enormity of what was said. Everyone sensed that something sacred happened that day. Interestingly, this was not a "church" group, but the Christian environment of this camp/retreat center made possible a way of relating that produced such trust.

Another word for trust is *faith*. Megan suffered senseless pain because of a chance encounter with a stranger. It may have resulted in a lifetime of fear, feeling that she was a victim of fate. The real turning point in her life came not on the day that she was molested, but on the day that her faith made her well—when a twist of fate became a twist of faith.

Megan is not the first woman to participate in her own healing by taking a risk. Consider Mark 5:25-34:

> Now there was a woman who had been suffering from hemorrhages for twelve years. She had endured much under many physicians, and had spent all that she had; and she was no better, but rather grew worse. She had heard about Jesus and came up behind him in the crowd and touched his cloak, for she said, "If I but touch his clothes, I will be made well." Immediately her hemorrhage stopped; and she felt in her body that she was healed of her disease. Immediately aware that power had gone forth from him, Jesus turned about in the crowd and said, "Who touched my clothes?" And his disciples said to him, "You see the crowd pressing in on you; how can you say, 'Who touched me?' " He looked all around to see who had done it. But the woman, knowing what had happened to her, came in fear and trembling, fell down before him, and told him the whole truth. He said to her, "Daughter, your faith has made you well; go in peace, and be healed of your disease."

Take a few minutes to consider the parallels between Megan's experience and the story from Mark's Gospel of the woman who reached out to Jesus.

• What role does *touch* play in the healing of these two women?

- How did the group participating in the ropes course become a channel of Christ's presence for Megan?
- What's the interplay between fear and trust in enhancing or deterring faith in God?
- How did each of these women tell the "whole truth" as part of their healing?
- Why do you think Jesus used the phrase, "Daughter, your faith has made you well; go in peace and be healed of your disease"?

When we talk about twists-of-faith ministry with youth, we mean helping youth reflect on their experiences in the light of God's presence and on how to live in response to that presence.

Providing this kind of spiritual leadership requires three things. First, the leader becomes aware of the experiences of the youth in his or her midst. Second, the leader recognizes connections between the young people's faith and their everyday experiences and helps them reflect on these experiences. Third, the leader is trustworthy. Youth will never invite into their lives in any significant way a leader whom they don't trust. Developing trust is the theme of this chapter, because trust is foundational to relationships and to faith.

Think deeply about the people you trust most. Write below the names of two people whom you would seek out in the midst of very difficult circumstances. Opposite each person's name list the characteristics and behaviors that draw you to him or her as a person worthy of your deepest trust.

NAME	CHARACTERISTICS AND BEHAVIORS
1.	
2.	

In his powerful book *The Seven Habits of Highly Effective People*[1], Stephen R. Covey discusses what it means to be trustworthy. In essence, there are ways of relating that build trust between people, and there are ways that destroy trust. Every time we choose how we will interact with people, we set in motion natural consequences or results. Even if we fail or refuse to choose and simply react to circumstances, we still cannot avoid the natural consequences of our actions.

It is crucial, therefore, that the spiritual leader who ministers with youth make deliberate choices about the way he or she will interact with youth both in the easy moments and

1 See *The Seven Habits of Highly Effective People*, by Stephen R. Covey (Simon & Schuster, 1989).

in the difficult times. The spiritual leader must recognize that circumstances do not force us to react in one way or the other. We have the power to choose. This is part of what it means to be made in God's image. We all know that choosing to interact positively in all circumstances is easier said than done. At the same time, the more we choose loving responses, the easier it becomes. Covey selects the word *habits* in the title of his book to emphasize the importance of practicing to choose well.

So what are the ways of relating that build trust? The truth is that you already know them. In fact, young children observe these ways and can name them. Try this little experiment. Think of two people you have met whom you do not trust. Why don't you trust them? What do they do or fail to do that makes it difficult for you to open yourself to them? Complete the sentence, "These people . . ." or "These people are . . . " For example: "These people berate my friends." "These people are dishonest." Or, "These people are distant." Now go beyond these two individuals and list more ways of interacting that hinder or undermine trust. Write these down under the column below titled "Trust Busters."

TRUST BUSTERS	TRUST BUILDERS

These negative examples also reveal the positive characteristics that build trust. Under the column titled "Trust Builders" and opposite each Trust Buster, write a word or phrase that describes its opposite. Positive influence with youth does not develop just because you are an adult or happen to be a leader. Authority is not the same as influence. Influence means that the youth consider what you do and say to be important enough that they continue to value it and to be shaped by it even when you are not around. They incorporate what they learn into their daily lives because they want to—which is good, because we cannot force this to happen. When youth experience the Spirit of God as a result of the way you relate with them, you gain influence.

Ways of relating that build lasting trust are from the Spirit. Listen to Paul's comments to the people of Galatia. In contrast to destructive behaviors, ". . . the fruit of the Spirit is love, joy, peace, patience, kindness, generosity, faithfulness, gentleness, and self-control. There is no law against such things . . . If we live by the Spirit, let us also be guided by the Spirit" (Galatians 5:22-23, 25). Paul may have mentioned other fruit of the Spirit, similar to some of those you generated under Trust Builders. If we hope to live out the fruit of the Spirit, it hinges on our willingness to be guided by the Spirit.

In part, being guided by the Spirit means learning to pause. Most of us understand the concept of stimulus and response—something happens, then we respond. This occurs every day in many forms. The element of that experience that often gets overlooked, however, is "sacred space." Imagine taking a moment, or perhaps a more extended period of time, and inserting it between what happens and your response to what happens. What you invite or bring into that sacred space greatly shapes everything that follows. Creating sacred space provides an opportunity to bring the fruit of the Spirit into the circumstances of our lives.

Sacred space allows us to participate with God in introducing love, gentleness, patience, and so forth, which releases divine energy. This frequently transforms not only our approach to a particular situation but also the repercussions and possibilities set in motion by the response we choose. Spiritual leaders can help create a different future for themselves and for the youth they serve by deliberately living out the principles of our faith rather than just reacting in kind to life's circumstances.

"Trust in the LORD with all your heart, and do not rely on your own insight. In all your ways acknowledge [God], and [God] will make straight your paths" (Proverbs 3:5-6). Pausing to invite the Spirit into the sacred space between what happens and how we respond is an affirmation of our trust in God. As our responses become more trustworthy through this practice, the youth will trust us more. It is important to be reminded that it also helps youth trust *God* more.

Does this mean that we need to be perfect to be spiritual leaders among youth? Of course not. Young people have a remarkable capacity to forgive and to understand the occasional less-than-perfect interactions. On the other hand, if our ways of interacting regularly contradict what we say we believe, youth will definitely take notice.

Skill and know-how also play a key role in establishing trust. Take a simple illustration. When my car needs to be repaired, I try to find a mechanic who is honest and caring. That is not enough, however. For me to trust the mechanic, he or she must also be skilled at repairing cars. The mechanic can be the most loving person in the world, but if he or she is not skilled at fixing automobiles, I am not going to take my car back repeatedly! Youth tend to trust adults who are lifelong learners willing to develop new skills related to youth ministry.

It is important, though, to keep in mind the picture of youth ministry as a whole. That is to say, adult leaders with youth also must seek to establish relationships of trust with all the people who care deeply about the young people whom the youth leaders serve. These people include the families of the youth, the faith community, the wider community, and the young people's friends. These are key people who can, and perhaps should, limit the youth leader's access to a teenager they care about when they are uncertain about how trustworthy the leader is. People trust a leader with youth when they know him or her to be a trustworthy person.

Anyone who works with youth on a long-term basis, either one-on-one or as part of a youth group, faces the potential of a situation in which the sense of trust between leader and youth is significantly damaged or questioned. Many of us know what that's like. Sometimes the concern causing the breakdown of trust is valid; in other cases, the concern arises out of incorrect, negative assumptions, or perhaps plain miscommunication. Whatever the scenario may be, trust is regained only through positive, shared experiences with those involved. This requires genuine humility and effort on the part of the adult leader. There are no easy alternatives. Ignoring, avoiding, or blaming on the part of the leader represents common attempts to relieve pressure, but such actions do not heal mistrust. Truthfully, it is much easier to maintain trust than it is to regain it.

All this talk about trust would be exaggerated were it not for the fact that some youth have real fears about the prospect of growing in faith. Moreover, being involved with an adult mentor or Christian youth group can be intimidating to some. Have you ever thought deeply about what these fears might be that some youth experience? Fear refers to the anxiety brought on by real pain or the worry about possible suffering. Adult leaders need to take the young people's misgivings seriously, even when the leaders may consider these unfounded. If a young person imagines that an experience might be uncomfortable for whatever reason, he or she fears that experience at some level. Even potentially meaningful experiences often produce apprehension. This includes being involved in developing a closer relationship with God.

Below is a list of issues about which youth typically experience anxiety. As an adult you may have some of these same fears. Even more, you may worry about making a mistake or handling a situation poorly. Don't let anxiety paralyze you. Grace abounds.

Fear Factors for Youth

The fear of being known. Human beings long to establish deep relationships with those who love them unconditionally. Human beings also dread the possibility that they might open themselves, only to be rejected. Youth wonder if they are really lovable, since they don't love everything they know about themselves. They fear that others might discover who they are, flaws and all, and that is scary, especially when those "others" are God or the people of God.

The fear of boredom. It's rough to commit yourself to or be required to suffer the uninteresting and unstimulating. Can you recall the weariness and monotony of such times in your own life? Youth consider it a big risk to chance such possible tedium. Unfortunately, the church has a reputation for sponsoring experiences that are less than engaging, intriguing, refreshing, inspiring, and animating. Honestly, though, some of the most enlivening and provocative experiences do occur in faith communities and youth ministries; so it is more than feasible to engage youth regularly at a level that energizes them. There will be boring sessions once in a while; this is normal. But what the youth really fear is constant boredom. Allow youth to participate in shaping their experience, and boring sessions will be far less likely.

The fear of unforeseen expectations. Youth sense that there is more than meets the eye in every new, significant venture they get involved in. They wonder, *What am I getting myself into? How hard will it be to get out of if I don't like it? If I join a Christian group, go to a camp sponsored by the church, or agree to explore faith with an adult mentor, what new responsibilities will I be pressured to take on? How much time will this really take? As I develop a deeper relationship with God and learn more about the Christian way of life, I may have new expectations of myself. I'm not sure I want that.*

The fear of restrictions. It's one thing to be invited into the freedom of exploring faith; it is quite another to feel that this is about yet another set of rules to "keep me in line." Youth are afraid that if they relate to the church, they will miss out on some of the best aspects of life. At a more practical level, there are only so many activities that any one person can participate in. Exploring faith restricts other options.

The fear of not knowing enough or not being capable. We sometimes overlook the trauma produced by feelings of embarrassment and inadequacy. Attempting new skills or experiences creates anxiety. The faith journey does involve new skills and adventures into the unknown. Being put on the spot to pray, when no one has ever shown you how to pray, may be embarrassing. Reading the Scriptures aloud might generate terror in the hearts of those who do not read well and those who have no idea how to even find a passage in the Bible. Simple things, like being laughed at in front of your peers, injure spirits. Youth want to succeed. They fear making mistakes or being unable to do what they are being asked to do. Most youth will dare to try, if they are helped to succeed.

The fear of being stereotyped. Teenagers struggle frequently with how their peers will react if they identify themselves as Christian. They worry that peers will judge them based on difficult encounters these friends have had with people who claim to be Christian but who are less than loving. People may stop inviting the teenager to parties or to other activities where the presence of a known Christian may cause some to feel uncomfortable. Youth worry that people will begin to stereotype them and will act differently toward them. They agonize about the possibility of rejection.

The fear of sharing or explaining one's faith. It stresses youth that someone may expect them to articulate a belief that they do not fully understand or that they remain uncertain about. They wonder how they can answer people who ask questions like, "How do you know God exists"? Feeling the need to defend their faith, even among other Christians, can be daunting for youth. It seems to them that it's important to know all the answers. Inviting others to church or youth group or sharing one's faith with other people can feel strange or even terrifying to think about, especially early on. They particularly want to avoid approaching others in ways that have offended them personally in the past.

The fear of family impact. Some teenagers hide significant difficulties in their own families. Getting close to others might expose these secrets. They are concerned that it would make things even worse if the church got involved. Some may even feel embarrassed or ashamed about unusual idiosyncrasies within their family that are not serious at all.

From a different angle, youth may fret about what will be required of their family if they get deeply interested and involved in exploring their faith. How much will it cost their family, both literally and figuratively? Will they need rides to and from youth events? How will involvement in church affect family schedules and time? Will the young person get support from family members, or will participation in church conflict with priorities and values held by the family? Will family members have different expectations of the young person because he or she is involved in spiritual growth?

The fear of manipulation. Most young people have heard about adults or groups who are not what they appear or claim to be. Although most youth give youth leaders the benefit of the doubt, some have good reason to be cautious. It's extremely painful to enter a relationship with a person or group under the guise of love and friendship, only to discover otherwise.

Our role as spiritual leaders is to help create an environment that is safe and trustworthy, so youth can move through some very real fears related to their faith journey. Our job is not to remove every challenge that might cause the young person to "stretch." True spiritual growth does bring about shifts in a person's perspective and priorities. Few people find this to be a totally comfortable experience. On the other hand, some of the fears listed above—for example, the fear of emotional manipulation—are caused by poor judgment on the part of adult leaders. However, adult leaders should certainly avoid exacerbating insecurities unnecessarily.

Ask yourself: What can I do that I'm not already doing that could help young people find relationships and have experiences that build their faith in God? This question deserves considerable time and thought. Read the passages from Scripture listed below. Then ask yourself: How can I support young people so that they can reflect on their lives and discover these biblical passages as not simply words on a page but as real in their lives? There are no magic formulas or set answers, because we must know the youth themselves and what they bring to the process.

- I sought the LORD, and [God] answered me, and delivered me from all my fears. (Psalm 34:4)

- It is the LORD who goes before you. [God] will be with you; [God] will not fail you or forsake you. Do not fear or be dismayed. (Deuteronomy 31:8)

- So do not worry about tomorrow, for tomorrow will bring worries of its own. Today's trouble is enough for today.   (Matthew 6:34)

- Who will separate us from the love of Christ? Will hardship, or distress, or persecution, or famine, or nakedness, or peril, or sword? . . . No, in all these things we are more than conquerors through him who loved us. For I am convinced that neither death, nor life, nor angels, nor rulers, nor things present, nor things to come, nor powers, nor height, nor depth, nor anything else in all creation, will be able to separate us from the love of God in Christ Jesus our Lord.   (Romans 8:35, 37-39)

The Importance of Community

It is important to mention the power that a loving community provides in helping young people move from fear to faith. Youth find great strength in knowing they are not in this endeavor alone. Interaction with adults and other youth who also consider spiritual growth important reassures and motivates them. One aspect of spiritual leadership is to provide opportunities for young people to participate in these types of communities, such as peer support groups, camp and retreat experiences, congregational life, family worship, and more. It may be necessary to help establish such communities for youth where these don't exist. If this is the case for you, it is important that you understand how lasting groups form.

Imagine group life to be like concentric rings of a tree. The outside layers protect the inner layers, where greater vulnerability exists. When young people have positive encounters at the "outer ring" of their experience, it encourages them to open themselves for encounters closer to the core of their being. It takes sensitivity as a spiritual leader to know where the group and individuals within the group are emotionally and spiritually, so that the process of increasing openness can proceed at an appropriate pace. Community life is quite dynamic, so incidents either within the group or beyond it may create a need to return to outer rings to regain trust.

1. *Information Exchange:* Most relationships begin with an exchange of non-threatening information such as names, interests, family configuration, hobbies, likes and dislikes, and so forth. There are lots of fun ways to do this; these are described in "icebreaker" books and other resources.

2. *Contact and Cooperation:* Appropriate touch creates a greater comfort level and sense of belonging. Even a simple touch such as playing tag or shaking hands is a way of

bonding. Cooperative projects or problem-solving activities require new levels of interaction that enhance friendship. Start out simply until the group is ready for more complex undertakings.

3. *Risk-Taking and Personal Disclosure:* It's often difficult for youth to go beyond their comfort zone if they haven't had some interaction at the first two levels. Even then, it may seem risky. Going rock climbing with a group or sharing some information about yourself that you don't want passed on to just anyone involves a greater level of trust. Many groups report great value in having members discuss what they need from one another before taking such 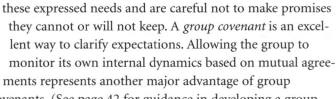 risks. Group members make promises to one another based on these expressed needs and are careful not to make promises they cannot or will not keep. A *group covenant* is an excellent way to clarify expectations. Allowing the group to monitor its own internal dynamics based on mutual agreements represents another major advantage of group covenants. (See page 42 for guidance in developing a group covenant.)

4. *Acceptance and Group Honesty:* It may seem odd to wait until this point to mention acceptance, but in a real way we cannot truly accept one another until we know one another at a significant level. True community involves great honesty in the midst of this acceptance. Love is not always easy. Most often we experience a shallow form of community characterized by feigned politeness, avoidance of conflict, lack of vulnerability, and a willingness to care only when it's to the advantage of group members to care. Such groups dissolve easily. They come and go often.

> I sought the LORD, and [God] answered me, and delivered me from all my fears.
>
> (Psalm 34:4)

Consider Jesus and the disciples as an example of a faith-forming community. They obviously loved one another and grew to accept one another. At the same time, there were moments of honesty that were difficult to face. For example, Jesus confronted the disciples about not allowing children access to him and denying them participation in his ministry. This confrontation was not comfortable, yet it was done in a caring manner. (See Luke 18:15-17.) Faith is formed when people can be real and loving with one another instead of pretending. Sometimes it takes knowing someone very well for a group to figure out what is the loving thing to do for that person and how to go about it—in other words, deciding what will truly nurture the person's soul.

5. *Sharing the Wellspring:* At some point a true faith community recognizes that it has tapped into an awesome, life-giving source—a Spirit as essential to life as water itself. People begin to celebrate the support, insights, and encouragement that come through true community. Gratitude and excitement well up and seek expression—an opportunity to flow out and be shared. This can take many forms. It may mean an effort where everyone works together to enrich the

world in some specific way or where group members support one another in their attempts to make a difference beyond the group. It may mean reaching out and inviting others into the group's experience. If members attempt to keep for themselves the indwelling of God's Spirit that they have received, the group will stagnate. The outward flow of the Spirit keeps community life healthy. Life seeks to bring life. Sometimes it takes great courage and faith to journey out into the world, but this work is crucial.

How can spiritual leaders help young people and groups move from fear to faith? They help by encouraging youth to seek God in the twists and turns of their lives and their relationships.

How to Develop a Group Covenant

STEP ONE: As leader, write down behaviors and attitudes that you have experienced in other effective, caring communities or groups. The list is for your reference only. It enables you to offer examples so that group members can understand the kind of input that is helpful.

STEP TWO: Have the group read Scriptures related to Christian community and loving relationships. List the key words and values mentioned. Reflect on this list while doing Step Three. Some possibilities are Genesis 9:8-17; 1 Corinthians 11:25 and 13:4-7; Romans 12:9-18; and Galatians 5:22-26 and 6:1-10.

STEP THREE: Ask group members to brainstorm and to share responses to the following questions and open-ended statements. Write all responses down on newsprint or dry-erase board for all to see.
- What mutual behaviors and attitudes would make this group the best it can be?
- To feel good about this group, I need other group members to . . .
- Group members can count on me to . . .
- The purpose or primary focus of this group is . . .

STEP FOUR: Review the responses with the group. Group items that are similar. Talk about the meaning behind suggestions that need clarification.

STEP FIVE: Discuss each item or group of items to determine whether every member is willing for that item or group of items to become a group norm. If so, the item or group of items becomes part of the group covenant. If there is not agreement on an item, revise it until it reflects a commitment that everyone can affirm; failing that, drop the item from the list.

STEP SIX: Refine the input to create a covenant that begins, "The purpose of our group (*insert the name of the group*) is . . ." Below the purpose statement is a second section that begins, "We as people of God agree to create a loving community by . . ." Below this statement, list the behaviors and attitudes that are shared group norms.

STEP SEVEN: Have the group review the statement. Make any final adjustments.

STEP EIGHT: Put the group covenant in a more permanent form that can be posted in common areas where all can see it and can be reminded of their commitments. Have each group member sign it. It's also helpful to have it in a form that can be distributed.

STEP NINE: Ask the group members to notice when they may not be fulfilling their covenant so the group can adjust its interactions to be faithful to one another.

A Group Covenant serves best when it fits on one side of a single sheet of 8 1/2-by-11 paper. A statement exceeding this length is unlikely to be used or remembered.

LEAD ON!

Young people need spiritual leaders! *Spiritual* refers to the sacred, the essence of life, the soul, the Holy Spirit, God. *Lead* means to serve others, to guide people toward a common destination, to influence, to proceed first, to focus on what is most important in a situation. Whether you are a parent, a grandparent, a caring adult, or a leader of youth, we urge you to be a spiritual leader for the young people in your midst. There are many ways to live out the call to be a spiritual leader. As a way to begin thinking about what it means to be a spiritual leader, reread the definitions of *spiritual* and *lead* above; then pause to reflect prayerfully on what God might be calling you to be and do.

You may be thinking, *Me, a spiritual leader for youth? I have too much to learn myself to lead anyone else. I'm not ready for that. I'm afraid I might make a mistake and influence a young person to take a wrong direction in life.* Or you may be saying to yourself, *I'm too old.* Or, *I'm too young and inexperienced.* Or even, *I don't have the talent or the time.*

We certainly empathize with your reservations about being a spiritual leader. We wrestle with the same doubts. It is a very humbling experience to recognize that God calls us to step out in faith to be leaders when often we do not feel totally comfortable with the idea.

We're in good company, however. The Bible recounts many stories about hesitant spiritual leaders. Check out the Book of Esther, which tells about a woman who anxiously stepped forward in dire circumstances to lead. What about Moses?

> But Moses said to God, "Who am I that I should go to Pharaoh . . . ?" [God] said, "I will be with you." . . . But Moses said to the LORD, "O my LORD, I have never been eloquent, neither in the past nor even now that you have spoken to your servant; but I am slow of speech . . . O my Lord, please send someone else."
>
> (Exodus 3:11, 12; 4:10, 13)

Certainly, one might think, an unscrupulous tax collector who had a reputation for deliberately cheating people would never become a spiritual leader; but people sat up and took notice of the transformed

Zacchaeus. After his encounter with Jesus he became an example of how to live faithfully (Luke 19:1-10). And how about lack of experience? Just read Jeremiah 1. Frankly, it's difficult to find examples of spiritual leaders who do not have moments of uncertainty, who are completely skilled and never make mistakes, and who constantly live in perfect harmony with God. At the same time, God continues to ask human beings to take leadership.

Leadership does not start with knowing it all; it begins with a consistent willingness to learn from God. Those who were closest to Jesus and who traveled with him were described as learners. The word *disciple* means student of a teacher. A key attribute of anyone who desires to lead youth toward a deeper faith in and relationship with God is a commitment to lifelong learning. Spiritual leaders intentionally enter a journey toward an ever-growing faith. If you feel that you have lots to learn about guiding youth on their faith journey, this affirms that you have the requisite humility to do so.

One Spiritual Leader's Story

Our local church begged for a volunteer to teach the Sunday school class for senior high youth. The call went out repeatedly, but no one stepped forward. This greatly disappointed us youth. Our patience was wearing thin. A bunch of teenagers actually wanted to study the Bible and learn; our parents and the church spurred us in this direction. But when we got excited about it, no adult would help. The irony was not lost on us, despite our age.

Finally, Bob spoke up at a church administrative board meeting. "We cannot let these kids down. They want to grow closer to God, and we need to respond. If no else will teach the class, I will." Teaching our class scared Bob to death. He had never taught a class of any kind in his entire life. None of the youth really knew him, so we were skeptical.

Frankly, the first few classes were beyond awful. Bob stammered and hesitated, and he didn't know how to lead discussions or engage the students. In general, he was a classic example of total disorganization. The youth rebelled. Without really conferring among ourselves we adopted a dual strategy of resistance through uncooperative silence mixed with occasional vocal barrages of discontent. We threatened to stop coming altogether. I am now ashamed to admit how cruel we were. We nearly had this grown man in tears.

One day, Bob pulled a couple of us aside after class. "Look," he said, "I'm not the best person to teach this class. You know it, and I know it. I feel like just quitting, because this is hard for me too. It's just too important to me to give up on this class. God is important. You youth are important. I'm a pretty simple kind of guy, and I don't know a lot about teaching. I'm doing a bad job—no denying that. Help me improve. Tell me what you need and want. I will keep showing up and will keep trying to do better. Even if no one comes, I will be here every week until this session of Sunday school ends."

You know what? Bob never improved all that much, but I never missed one of his classes. His sincere love for God and for youth taught me more than a year's worth of Sunday school classes could. As long as he showed up, I showed up too. Later that year, Bob moved away because of a job change. I never saw him again. His example travels with me, though. He taught me about faithfulness, grace, and accepting even imperfection as a gift. I thank God for you, Bob, wherever you may be. You taught me a lot about what it means to follow Christ.

Now the eleven disciples went to Galilee, to the mountain to which Jesus had directed them. When they saw him, they worshiped him; but some doubted. And Jesus came and said to them, "All authority in heaven and on earth has been given to me. Go therefore and make disciples of all nations, baptizing them in the name of the Father and of the Son and of the Holy Spirit, and teaching them to obey everything that I have commanded you. And remember, I am with you always, to the end of the age." (Matthew 28:16-20)

REFLECT ON THIS PASSAGE OF SCRIPTURE USING THE FOLLOWING QUESTIONS:

What implications does this passage have for ministry with youth?

What support does Jesus offer when he sends "disciples" to "make disciples"?

Spiritual Leadership and Spiritual Practices

Youth do not demand perfection from adults. They only expect adults to be sincere and to be practicing disciples *themselves*. As we said, a spiritual leader is first and foremost a disciple—a companion of Christ who lives out the teachings of the faith and who assists in spreading these teachings.

David Lowes Watson, author of *Covenant Discipleship*, describes discipleship as a state of being "open to God's grace."[1] Grace is God's constant, active invitation to be in loving, life-giving,

---

1 *Covenant Discipleship: Christian Formation through Mutual Accountability,* by David Lowes Watson (Discipleship Resources, 1991); p. 17.

and transforming relationship with us. Our Creator offers us channels or ways to participate in strengthening our relationship with God. John Wesley, the visionary leader who helped shape the movement that ultimately led to the establishment of The United Methodist Church, identified some of these ways to God. He called them "means of grace."[2] Since spiritual leadership depends upon a vital connection with God, these practices (or means of grace), along with other spiritual disciplines, have long characterized the Christian life.

Practice refers to a repeated course of action or way of doing things, which eventually becomes a habit. Practice is not always easy. It has highs and lows. Some days, even the best athletes, musicians, and artists make the effort to practice rather reluctantly. They continue, though, because the discipline of regular practice is essential for all proficient leaders in any endeavor. The reward for these leaders is the joy of experiencing that to which they give themselves. In the case of spiritual leaders, we experience God, to whom we give ourselves by dedicating our time and loving effort to that relationship.

The practice of spiritual discipline means engaging in a regular focus on God and on the ways of Christ until these become part of our nature—a way of life. All meaningful relationships, without exception, require attentiveness and spending time together. It's a simple, straightforward truth that we all know by experience. The same holds for our connection with God. Initially, it may feel like an interruption to undertake new spiritual practices, because it requires us to put forth some energy, to change, to discontinue some life patterns and to take up new ones. (But what relationship doesn't make demands?) Spiritual practices— means of grace—are not ways to earn God's love; rather, they are expressions of God's love, coming to us in the form of opportunities to grow closer to God. We simply need to walk these paths regularly—and so discover anew the Heart of life itself.

As spiritual leaders, we effectively guide youth only when we ourselves walk the paths of faithful discipleship. A path to God is created by walking along it. It's vital to realize that we prepare youth to be disciples of *Christ*, not of us. Spiritual leadership centers on guiding young people to experience and to grow closer to Christ. This is much easier to accomplish if leaders with youth are also experiencing and growing closer to God.

Spiritual Practices as Pathways to God

The remainder of this chapter describes practices that hosts of people personally identify as avenues to God. We begin with a discussion of some of the means of grace identified by John Wesley; then we explore other methods to open ourselves to the Spirit. Consider carefully each of these practices and methods. You may be engaging in a number of these already and yet yearn for an even deeper connection with God. Or you may be challenged to adopt some of these activities for the first time. Great! The list below is not meant to be exhaustive, but rather to spark possibilities.

2 See John Wesley's sermon, "The Means of Grace," in *The Works of John Wesley Volume V* (Zondervan Publishing House, n.d.); pp. 185-201.

Imagine trying to reach a destination by taking a step only once in a while. You may never get there. Wesley and other great spiritual leaders consider it a necessity to actively and consistently participate in a combination of spiritual disciplines. Rarely does one path by itself suffice. The important thing is to pursue these practices intentionally, to keep focused on God, and to live the way of love.

The Means of Grace Identified by John Wesley

As we said above, John Wesley discovered a number of spiritual disciplines—"channels" or "means" of grace—for deepening our relationship with God. We have selected and expanded on a few of these to help you grow as a spiritual leader of youth.

Prayer (private, family, public)
> *Intent of prayer:* To communicate with God
> *Benefits of prayer:* Providing opportunities to listen for God's direction and desire; building a stronger relationship with God; requesting support for ourselves and for others; expressing thanks and appreciation for God's presence and gifts; seeking reconciliation with God and others; uniting in prayer with other people of faith around the world.
> *Approaches to prayer:*
> - *Have a spontaneous response:* As you recognize feelings—positive or negative—talk with God about them at that moment.
> - *Pray the prayers of other people:* Participate in prayer led by others or inspired by their situation. Read the heartfelt prayers written by others, such as the prayer of Saint Francis, the Lord's Prayer, or modern prayers.
> - *Pray with the family:* Bless meals; join children in a prayer at bedtime; celebrate times of joy in the family; look for God's wisdom in difficult situations.
> - *Plan a personal quiet time:* Set aside time each day for silence and for dialogue with God.
> - *Take part in corporate prayer:* Gather and pray with other believers in group settings.

> ### Searching the Scriptures
> *Intent of searching the Scriptures:* To learn more about the Christian faith by reflecting upon the encounters people of the Bible had with God and how they interpreted these encounters.
> *Benefits of searching the Scriptures:* Hearing the good news of God's presence with us in Jesus Christ through the power of the Holy Spirit; learning what Jesus taught his disciples about how to live, along with the biblical authors' own reflections on the Christian life; discovering the importance and nature of Christian community; encountering many examples of disciples practicing the spiritual disciplines.

Approaches to searching the Scriptures:
- *Use personal study guides:* Follow the Revised Common Lectionary, which takes a person through the majority of the Bible in a three-year cycle.
- *Take part in a group study:* Use a resource like the DISCIPLE Bible Study; or gather folks for a Bible study you designed.
- *Listen to tapes:* Take advantage of time riding in the car or exercising by listening to a Bible study or the Bible itself being read on the tapes.
- *Use a topical Bible study:* Use resources such as a concordance or Bible dictionary to study Scripture passages that have a common theme, such as hope or God's love.
- *Prepare presentations, resources, or programs:* These could be for a church school class, a youth-group study, a sermon, or an article—any presentation, resource, or program that incorporates scriptural insights.

Celebrating the Lord's Supper

Intent of celebrating the Lord's Supper: With thanksgiving to remember or to "relive" with the community of faith Christ's loving sacrifice for the world and to find nourishment for the life of discipleship.

Benefits of celebrating the Lord's Supper: Expressing and participating in our unity in Christ; renewing our faith; reconciling ourselves to God and to others and finding forgiveness; following Christ's guidance to share this meal as a family of faith; remembering the history of God's love for us; making use of a regular opportunity to experience Christ's presence in our lives.

Approaches to celebrating the Lord's Supper:
- *Receive Holy Communion regularly:* Settings include congregational worship, camps or retreats, and family gatherings. In celebrating the Lord's Supper in these settings, be conscious of what is said and done so that you can participate more fully in the meaning of Holy Communion.
- *Prepare the Communion elements:* Lay out the Lord's Table for public worship; make the bread and provide the juice or wine; clean and prepare the Communion ware and utensils for the next worship service.
- *Write prayers and liturgy:* These can be used as words of hope and affirmation during Communion.
- *Engage in prayer:* Pray with people who request prayer after receiving Communion; kneel at the altar for personal prayer; or pray silently, either in the pew or at the altar, for the people as they receive Communion.
- *Distribute the Communion elements:* Assist in distributing the bread and cup.
- *Take Communion to others:* Participate in taking Communion to individuals who are ill or who are unable to leave home.
- *Create opportunities to celebrate Communion:* Plan opportunities to celebrate Communion with youth—for example, during a youth-group meeting or at a retreat.

- *Receive Communion in other churches:* Attend Communion services in other denominations. Participating in the wider fellowship of Christ's body through Communion may nurture your spirit in new ways.

Fasting

Intent of fasting: To give up food, or something else of value, for a specific period of time to better understand and to participate in Christ's sacrifice for the world; and to learn to depend on God as the source of life.

Benefits of fasting: Heightening awareness of the needs of others; experiencing the pain and discomfort of living without some of life's necessities in order to appreciate what God provides; learning to depend more upon God than upon human forms of security; using the time or resources normally spent on the activity from which one is abstaining to intentionally connect with God and to apply the resources to meet the needs of others; living more simply; learning to give without receiving a reward.

Approaches to fasting:

- *Go without food:* Choose a specific time frame for abstaining from food. During the time you would normally spend on eating, focus on spiritual growth.
- *Go without a purchase:* Instead of buying an item you desire, divert the resources to the needs of other people, of society, or of the earth.
- *Go without an activity:* Take television as an example. Many of us enjoy watching a lot of television. Reduce the time and energy set aside for watching television. Divert the extra time and energy to activities that are fulfilling and that make an impact. Some folks ride bikes and walk instead of driving a car, because it is more gentle on the earth and good for themselves both physically and spiritually.
- *Go without possessions:* Give away things you own, share them, or loan them out as an expression of loving community.

Christian Conversation

Intent of Christian conversation: To develop a relationship with a person or a group of people by meeting regularly for mutual encouragement, support, and accountability with a view to growing and living more faithfully as people of God.

Benefits of Christian conversation: Gleaning the wisdom of others; expanding your self-understanding and understanding God's desires for your life; supporting others by listening; gaining motivation to live more lovingly and faithfully; revealing your thoughts and feelings; overcoming the tendency to rationalize important issues in your life, through the reflection of caring people who know you; establishing goals for spiritual growth, undergirded by the promise to be held accountable by another person or by a group of people.

Approaches to Christian conversation:
- *Make a spiritual friend:* Identify one friend in the faith with whom you can share regularly and from whom you can seek guidance and support.
- *Start or join a Covenant Discipleship Group:* The purpose of a Covenant Discipleship Group is to help people grow spiritually in and practice faithfully the core of their beliefs.
- *Find a spiritual director:* Seek out a person who can help you develop a plan for your spiritual growth and who will meet with you to discuss your progress. This usually means that the person you choose as spiritual director should have a mature faith and perhaps specialized training.
- *Reflect on decisions:* When important decisions arise, ask other people to reflect with you on the ramifications of each decision, and to help identify sources of spiritual wisdom, so that you can discern the desire of God for your life.

Doing No Harm

Intent of doing no harm: To avoid or to cease behaviors that harm or block positive possibilities; to abandon conduct that separates you from God.
Benefits of doing no harm: Preventing the suffering that follows negative interactions or poor judgment; confessing faults and forgiving as a first step toward new ways of being Christian; enhancing harmony with God, your own soul, and with others; spending time productively instead of creating problems for yourself and for others.
Approaches to doing no harm:
- *Examine yourself:* Listen with greater awareness to your "inner voice"— your conscience—when you feel uneasy, ashamed, or in the wrong. Honestly take stock of your behavior, discerning whether your behavior is causing the Spirit to warn you. If so, commit yourself to making better choices; then follow through.
- *Invite honesty:* Invite people whom you respect and trust deeply to identify behaviors in your life that may be destructive. After all, the truth sets us free. Many people, including John Wesley, have engaged in this kind of honest sharing for the sake of their spiritual growth. Listen to some of the questions regularly asked in the small groups Wesley created: ". . . What have you thought, said, or done, of which you doubt whether it be sin or not? . . . Do you desire we should tell you whatsoever we think, whatsoever we fear, whatsoever we hear, concerning you? . . . Do you desire that, in doing this, we should come as close as possible, that we should cut to the quick, and search your heart to the bottom?"[3]
- *Listen to voices calling for justice:* Some harm is caused by the combined and accepted behavior of large groups of people of which we may be a

3 "Rules of the Band-Societies," *The Works of John Wesley Volume VIII* (Zondervan Publishing House, n.d.); p. 273.

part. Open yourself to learning from those in touch with suffering, and from those who are calling us to a broader vision of community and mutual concern. Study these voices, not to be obsessed by guilt but to find new avenues for avoiding harm.

Doing Good

Intent of doing good: To practice the love of Christ through right actions.

Benefits of doing good: Bringing joy to God and others; living out our essential nature as people made in God's image; fulfilling Jesus' commandment to love one another as he loved us; developing sensitivity to the physical and spiritual needs of others; producing the fruit of the Spirit: "love, joy, peace, patience, kindness, generosity, faithfulness, gentleness, and self-control" (Galatians 5:22).

Approaches to doing good:
- *Help social service agencies:* Volunteer to help in some way, and share your resources where they are needed most.
- *Be a good neighbor:* Get to know your neighbors and support them.
- *Help bear the burdens of others in the community of faith:* Share your talents, presence, and resources among those in the Christian fellowship.
- *Follow the examples mentioned in Scripture:* Many passages in the Bible name acts of doing good—for example, visiting the sick and imprisoned, giving food to the hungry, and forgiving one another. Read these biblical examples and follow them.
- *Become aware of points of great need worldwide:* If at all possible, visit some of these places around the world to serve and/or support the work of others.

Corporate Worship

Intent of corporate worship: To gather as the body of Christ to meet God and to celebrate God's presence.

Benefits of corporate worship: Joining other believers to hear the voice of God; publicly giving and receiving forgiveness; gaining spiritual renewal through music, ritual, and prayer; considering interpretations of God's Word for our own time; lifting up joys, concerns, and signs of God's presence in our daily lives; thanking God for many gifts and for life itself; renewing our dedication to live as Christ's disciples in the world.

Approaches to corporate worship:
- *Attend worship regularly:* Find a local community of faith, or establish one; then attend often.
- *Enhance worship:* Join leaders to design forms of worship that are relevant and powerful.
- *Invite others to worship:* Ask people not attending a church to worship with you. Assist them in getting established within the fellowship.

- *Participate as a leader in worship:* Read Scripture, preach, offer music (if that's your gift), or step forward in other ways to serve the congregation's worship life.

Other Pathways

Meditation/Practicing God's Presence

Intent of meditation: To hone the capacity to focus on God and to hear the voice of God.

Benefits of meditation: Slowing down and experiencing increased peace and awareness of what is truly important, regardless of the situation; letting go of distractions that obstruct full attentiveness to the present moment; repeating simple sacred phrases or passages (see below) as a way to shape faith; maintaining a connection with God throughout the day's activities.

Approaches to meditation:

- *Find a mentor or a written guide to meditation:* Seek out a person or a resource that teaches the techniques of meditation. This person or resource does not need to be Christian; for example, Buddhists value and practice meditation. You can learn the process and techniques of meditation and then adapt these by incorporating Christian themes and understandings that are meaningful to you.
- *Practice breath prayers:* Designate a place in your home and a time to engage in complete solitude. Sit comfortably in an upright position that keeps you relaxed yet attentive. Close your eyes and begin to concentrate on your breathing, taking note of each inhale and exhale. This is the very breath of life itself, which comes from God. (The word in the Old Testament for *spirit* also means "wind" or "breath.") Breathe slowly until you are able to concentrate on each inhale and exhale; then begin to breathe a phrase. For example, while inhaling, think of the phrase, "Bless the Lord"; while exhaling, think of the phrase, "Oh my soul." While inhaling the second time, think or speak the phrase, "All that is within me"; while exhaling the second time, ponder the phrase, "Bless God's holy name." Repeat this pattern, which is adapted from Psalm 103:1, over and over until it becomes a part of who you are. You can choose any simple phrase or write your own.
- *Practice memorization:* Memorize scriptural passages, prayers (such as the prayer of St. Francis of Assisi, page 68), songs, poetry, or any other meaningful writings. Recite them aloud or in your mind. Memorize something new each week.

Retreat Into Nature

Intent of retreating into nature: To escape the normal routine of daily life for an extended period of spiritual growth in a setting of natural beauty.

Benefits of retreating into nature: Opening yourself to new encounters with God and to fresh perspectives on Christian faith and life; experiencing renewal, healing, and peace through the power of creation; getting acquainted with others at a deeper level through Christian group-retreats and camps; leaving behind the hurriedness and distractions of daily life.

Approaches to retreating into nature:

- *Attend camps and retreats:* Many denominations sponsor such events on a regular basis; information is readily available at regional offices. Other organizations in your area may sponsor similar events to nurture faith.
- *Spend time in creation:* In John 1:1, 3 we read, "In the beginning was the Word, and the Word was with God, and the Word was God. . . . All things came into being through [the Word] . . ." God speaks to us through creation if only we will listen.
- *Go on personal retreats:* Plan time alone for spiritual growth, prayer, and study; or go to a center designed for personal retreats.

Journaling and Writing Letters

Intent of journaling and writing letters: To record feelings and reflections so they can be reviewed to foster spiritual growth.

Benefits of journaling and writing letters: Seeing things more clearly through the process of writing; bearing your soul in God's presence; rereading what was written, even years later, to gain insight and celebrate growth; communicating thoughts more concisely with select friends.

Approaches to journaling and writing letters:

- *Maintain a journal:* Regularly (daily or weekly) record with utter honesty experiences, thoughts, and feelings. These are for your eyes only, unless you choose to share them. After each entry, spend time in conversation with God about these things.
- *Write letters that build relationships:* Send letters of reconciliation, appreciation, inspiration, encouragement, and so forth. Such letters often have a profound impact on both the one who writes and the one who receives the letter. Also, a letter is something tangible that can be kept.
- *Maintain a "grateful journal":* Each day, record four or more things for which to thank God. Begin each entry by writing, "God, thank you for . . ." This is a simple thing to do; yet people attest to the life-transforming power of this practice.
- *Seek wisdom and support:* Choose a trusted mentor(s) or friend(s) who is wise. Negotiate with him or her to be in dialogue through letters or e-mail either on a regular basis or during times of need. This person's role would be to read your correspondence and to reflect upon it, and then to write back.
- *Keep a journal of inspirational items:* Record songs, poetry, or passages that touch you deeply. Also record moments in your life that have a particular impact upon you. You can return to these from time to time for spiritual renewal and inspiration. What a great collection to pass on to future generations.

Study and Devotional Reading

Intent of study and devotional reading: To expand your understanding and ability through learning new insights from books and resources beyond the Bible, with a view to living more faithfully as a member of God's people.

Benefits of study and devotional reading: Exposure to new discoveries from many fields of study such as physics, business, education, and so forth, that will enlighten you; reducing the tendency to put false limits on what is sacred; recognizing new ways to connect faith to the dimensions of everyday life; learning from people who live in different places and who have life experiences very different from yours; taking advantage of a wide variety of devotional resources.

Approaches to study and devotional reading:

- *Read with faith connections in mind:* Many authors in a variety of fields of study talk about concepts that have spiritual implications. For example, observant Christians can hardly fail to notice the spiritual basis of many of the concepts expressed in Steven Covey's book *The Seven Habits of Highly Effective People,* a book written primarily as a business management resource. As you read books, listen to cassette tapes, and watch videos, begin to develop eyes and ears to hear the voice of God in these resources.
- *Subscribe to a devotional resource:* Your denomination, book catalogues, or local bookstores provide many devotional materials. Seek them out and use them regularly.
- *Start a reading/study group:* Enjoy dialogue with others who are studying the same material you are. Or invite a few friends or colleagues to join you in studying and discussing resources all of you find meaningful so as to enhance spiritual growth. Studying as a group also increases the likelihood that the practice will continue, since participants make a commitment to others.

Music and the Arts

Intent of music and the arts: To live as a co-creator with God; to experience the inspiration of God through arts that reflect different aspects of life.

Benefits of music and the arts: Being moved and inspired by art, drama, and music at the core of one's being; communicating with God through expressions that go beyond words; creating gifts that can be offered to God and to others; gaining new appreciation for the wonder and sacredness of beauty; allowing art to comfort you or to disturb your complacency.

Approaches to music and the arts:

- *Make a "joyful noise":* Join a choir; play an instrument; participate in musical theater; dance; or write songs.
- *Create hands-on expressions:* Draw covers for bulletins; paint; make banners; do a mosaic out of broken ceramic tile; sculpt items for worship centers; make altar cloths or stoles; create a slide presentation; make objects that move people to a new awareness of God and the Christian

life; offer whatever art form you enjoy as a gift to the community or to the people you love.

- *Create a scene!:* Join or start a drama group; lead an arts camp; deliver a sermon; perform readings or poetry; attend drama performances by your youth; start a Sunday school class for the purpose of discussing the spiritual themes found in movies; do role-plays as a teaching method; portray people you admire for an audience; and so forth.

Renewal and Self-Care[4]

Intent of renewal and self-care: To love yourself and to maintain the necessary balance to ensure a joyful, productive life.
Benefits of renewal and self-care: Regenerating the physical, mental, and spiritual resources needed to function effectively over the long run.
Approaches to renewal and self-care:

- *Care for the physical:* Exercise regularly; get plenty of sleep and make room for relaxation; watch your nutrition; enjoy outdoor activities.
- *Care for relationships:* Spend time with people who nurture your soul; join a club or interest group; heal a broken relationship or end a destructive relationship; create fun experiences with family or friends.
- *Learn new things:* Connect with new ideas that inspire and motivate you; take up or reactivate a skill or hobby you enjoy; attend workshops and continuing education events; spend time with a mentor (this may even be the writings of an historical figure); scan the New York bestseller list for inspiring books to read.

> Give yourself a gift! Begin a new spiritual practice as a pathway to God.

- *Care for the spiritual:* Reconnect with your core values and the defining experiences of your faith; visit the people and places that had a profound effect on your spiritual journey; participate in a faith community; practice the spiritual disciplines—the "means of grace."

So What? Now What?

Reading this chapter may bring you knowledge, but fail to lead you closer to God in any real way. If these pages are going to help you grow closer to God, two things must happen. Both are things that only you can implement.

First, the practices described in this chapter become spiritual practices only when you seek the Spirit intentionally through them. One can engage in all these disciplines and not grow closer to God or become more loving, if one's

4 Material in this section adapted from *The Seven Habits of Highly Effective People,* by Stephen R. Covey (Simon and Schuster, 1989), especially p. 288.

motivation is not inspired by the Spirit. So constantly practice the presence of God. Seek to live the way of Christ.

Second, it does little good to choose a path and then not take it. This is why these routes to God are called "spiritual practices." Unlocking the mystery of these paths comes only through repeated journeying along them. Practicing takes time, consistency, and repetition.

You have an opportunity to give yourself a gift. Review and prayerfully consider the spiritual pathways described in this chapter. Choose one or two of these practices—ones that you are not now doing—that you feel would make a significant difference in your spiritual life. Commit yourself to engaging in this spiritual practice, either daily or weekly, for a set length of time. Allow yourself enough time; it takes a while to establish a habit of faith.

Linking with God through these spiritual practices will not only feed your soul and guide you; it will also feed and guide your ministry with youth. So lead on!

it's BEYOND ME!

One of the greatest gifts you can bestow upon yourself and your youth is this truth: You are not alone! Granted, you may at times feel alone or think you are alone in your efforts to nurture the spirit of young people. But this sense of isolation is an illusion; it isn't real. So many adult workers with youth become demoralized, burned out—even resentful—because they begin to believe they are on their own in ministry.

Inevitably, as a spiritual leader among youth, you will run into circumstances beyond your comfort level or abilities. Don't be surprised. When it does happen, work through these situations by leaning on supplemental sources of help. Those who rely solely on their own capabilities often end up overwhelmed.

We're told that on average a youth worker lasts between twelve and eighteen months in an assignment. Unfortunately, this is just about the time the youth worker is beginning to gain the trust of the teenagers and to exercise the kind of positive influence that would reap huge benefits had he or she continued. That is why it is so important to identify sources of help now so that when you are truly in need, you can tap them. Avoid burnout. Remember, you are not alone.

Listen to the Word: "So I say to you, Ask, and it will be given you; search, and you will find; knock, and the door will be opened for you. For everyone who asks receives, and everyone who searches finds, and for everyone who knocks, the door will be opened" (Luke 11:9-10). So ask, search, and knock until you find the support network necessary. You may not find it in the first place you look or even in the place you'd expect to find it—but God is faithful.

You Are Not Alone!

We suggest four categories of assistance and support: God, people, organizations, and resources. God is a "very present help in trouble" (Psalm 46:1b); so go to God. Other human beings possess awesome capacities for encouragement, know-how, and assistance. Organizations specialize in particular areas; therefore, they can offer concise, written resources and human networks related to their specialty. Numerous resources exist for those willing to search.

The charts that follow list some alternatives under each of the categories—God, people, organizations, and resources—to stimulate brainstorming. We hope you will add your own insights to these options, and fill in the specifics in the spaces provided or on a separate sheet of paper. It's crucial for you to determine what kind of support best suits your particular circumstances and setting. We can't predict all the variables of your situation; therefore, we can't give you pat answers. We can, however, provide a process to get you started. Your backup network may change from time to time depending on the issues you face. Use the following charts whenever you feel the need to broaden your web of support, or when caring people urge you to do so.

I AM NOT ALONE: GOD

Specific pathways to God I choose in seeking support for this situation are . . .
(See Chapter 4, Lead On!)

PATHWAYS

❏ Prayer (private, family, corporate)

❏ Searching the Scriptures

❏ Celebrating the Lord's Supper

❏ Fasting

❏ Christian Conversation

❏ Doing No Harm

❏ Doing Good

❏ Corporate Worship

❏ Meditation/Practicing God's Presence

❏ Retreat Into Nature

❏ Journaling and Writing Letters

❏ Study and Devotional Reading

❏ Music and the Arts

❏ Renewal and Self-Care

❏ Other: _____

I AM NOT ALONE: OTHER PEOPLE

PEOPLE

- ❏ Friends
- ❏ Pastors
- ❏ Other Youth Leaders
- ❏ Extended Family Members
- ❏ Medical Personnel
- ❏ Counselors
- ❏ Legal Advisors
- ❏ Other Religious Leaders
- ❏ Educators
- ❏ Trained Activity Specialists
- ❏ Parents
- ❏ Retirees
- ❏ The Youth
- ❏ Denominational Staff
- ❏ Neighbors
- ❏ Coworkers
- ❏ Church Members
- ❏ Other: _____

People to contact for the situation I'm facing now:

Name: _____

Contact Information: _____

_____

Type of Support: _____

. . .

Name: _____

Contact Information: _____

_____

Type of Support: _____

. . .

Name: _____

Contact Information: _____

_____

Type of Support: _____

I AM NOT ALONE: ORGANIZATIONS

ORGANIZATIONS

- ❏ Crisis Hotlines
- ❏ Community Service Groups
- ❏ Foundations
- ❏ Schools
- ❏ Religious Institutions
- ❏ Government Agencies
- ❏ Parent-Family Support Groups
- ❏ Youth Clubs and Agencies
- ❏ Family Planning Clinics
- ❏ Recreational Programs and Centers
- ❏ Stores
- ❏ Libraries
- ❏ Speaker Bureaus
- ❏ Chamber of Commerce
- ❏ Low-Income Services
- ❏ Camps and Retreat Centers
- ❏ Corporations
- ❏ Museums, Zoos, Community Theater
- ❏ Peer Support Groups
- ❏ Associations and Fellowships
- ❏ Other: _____

Organizations to contact for the situation I'm facing now:

Name: _____

Contact Information: _____

_____

Type of Support: _____

. . .

Name: _____

Contact Information: _____

_____

Type of Support: _____

. . .

Name: _____

Contact Information: _____

_____

Type of Support: _____

I AM NOT ALONE: RESOURCES

RESOURCES

- ❏ Books
- ❏ Internet
- ❏ Catalogues
- ❏ Magazines
- ❏ Audiotapes
- ❏ Videotapes
- ❏ Fundraising/Donations
- ❏ Arts and Crafts Supplies
- ❏ Free Local Attractions
- ❏ The Natural World
- ❏ Electronic Equipment
- ❏ Policies and Guidelines
- ❏ Food
- ❏ Musical Instruments/Songbooks
- ❏ Games
- ❏ Symbols
- ❏ Objects for Object Lessons
- ❏ Photographs
- ❏ Recreation Equipment
- ❏ Other: _____

Resources to aid in the situation I'm facing now:

Specific type of resource desired: _____

Where I might find the resource:

_____

_____

• • •

Specific type of resource desired: _____

Where I might find the resource:

_____

_____

• • •

Specific type of resource desired: _____

Where I might find the resource:

_____

_____

Indicators for When to Seek Help

By now it should be clear that you are not alone. It is really a matter of choosing to seek support when you need it. How do you know when it is prudent to seek additional help? Most of us are more capable than we feel, so sometimes it may be difficult to discern when a situation reaches beyond our capabilities. However, when one or more of the following indicators appears in a situation you're facing, let it be a catalyst for at least asking the question, "Is this situation beyond me?"

- *Intuition:* The feeling or sense that additional assistance is important to deal with a particular situation.
- *Legal or policy implications:* It is critical to request advice when legal issues or policy guidelines may apply to the situation.
- *Personal issues or struggles:* Youth may be wrestling with issues that elicit strong reactions within you as a leader, because you may not have resolved similar issues in your own life. When this occurs, it is extremely difficult to be objective, spiritually centered, and truly focused on the young person rather than on yourself.

- *Lack of knowledge or skill:* Sometimes we simply don't know enough to deal adequately with a particular situation. This is a clue to find someone who has the knowledge needed, or to enter a learning process to gain the knowledge or skill ourselves.
- *Impact on other people:* If a situation will have a significant impact on people beyond yourself and the youth, then discern carefully who else should be informed or involved.
- *Becoming worn out:* Leaders can at times become too tired to be effective and need someone else to take over.
- *Judgment being questioned:* Occasionally, you may make a poor decision, or someone may simply disagree with what you have done in a particular situation. Either way, the scrutiny of your leadership will increase for a period of time. In such a case, it is wise to consult with trusted advisors, especially when other potentially delicate situations arise during this time of increased scrutiny.
- *Health and safety:* Parents and church leaders expect youth leaders to guard the health and safety of young people at all times. There is little tolerance when leaders ignore this foundational level of caring. Be sure you understand health and safety risks and follow proper procedures.
- *Young people with extensive needs:* Long-term challenges or multiple difficulties sometimes require additional adult interaction and/or help from people beyond your immediate group of leaders.
- *Inability of a young person to relate to the youth director:* This does not necessarily imply that the youth dislikes you; he or she may simply feel more comfortable interacting with another adult. Besides, one adult can relate in a significant way to only a limited number of youth at a given time. That is why it is important to have other adults, besides you, available to interact with the youth.
- *Working with a team:* Working together as a team may involve multiple people having to participate in making a decision or in responding to a situation. Alternatively, the team may choose to respond individually to the situation and then to provide team members with the necessary information. Either way, it is important to be clear about the process to follow.
- *Additional adult help required:* Some activities require additional help. For example, you may need drivers—or a driver with a special driver's license classification—for a mission trip. You may need a certain number of adults to meet ratio guidelines, and so forth. Some efforts hinge on the assistance of others.

Staying Out of Trouble

In addition to being sensitive about when to secure appropriate assistance, spiritual leaders need to steer clear of creating unnecessary complications in carrying out their ministry with youth. If you're not careful, you can easily make challenges far more complex than they really are. Doing this diverts attention from fulfilling your ministry because you add unnecessary issues to resolve.

To avoid getting entangled in needless complications, follow the seven guide-lines below. You will be happier—and so will those around you!

1. *Promise confidentiality only when it's appropriate.* Many sincere leaders put themselves in a moral dilemma by promising confidentiality before they even know the nature of what is going to be discussed. Some information should be passed on to other people, when appropriate. Sometimes this is what loving a particular young person requires. For example, you may promise a teenager to hold in confidence whatever he or she shares with you. However, what do you do when, afterwards, this same teenager tells you that he or she plans to commit suicide? Or what if he or she describes an abusive situation that the law requires you to report? Trust is under-mined because you gave your word prematurely.

2. *Hold private conversations in public settings, if at all possible.* Unfortunately, misunderstandings and/or accusations can arise if we repeatedly meet with individual youth behind closed doors or out of the view of others. These incidents can damage your reputation and effectiveness, even if the claims are not true. Understandably, the youth will receive the benefit of the doubt in such a situation, since he or she is perceived as having less power than you. Awareness of the possibility of such incidents takes on even greater import when you meet with people of the opposite sex.

3. *Remember to live faithfully.* Actions speak louder than words, so be a faith-ful role model. Duplicity eats away at trust and respect.

4. *Pursue understanding and offer compassion.* It's tempting to react in kind. So when you feel you are being attacked, the inclination is to attack in return; when you feel you are being blamed, the tendency is to return the blame. You may even try to recruit people to take your side so you can "win." Spiritual leadership calls us to maturity. This means participating in securing a loving outcome to a situa-tion of conflict rather than reacting defensively. Mature spiritual leaders exchange fear and insecurity for a deep desire to understand the pain or concern behind someone else's behavior that the leader experiences as hurtful. Compassion grows in the soil of understanding.

> God is our refuge and strength, a very present help in trouble.
>
> (Psalm 46:1)

5. *Establish helpful guidelines.* Such a process includes formulating group covenants about how people are to treat and encourage one another; using dis-cipline as a process of learning rather than solely as punishment; agreeing on a process for conflict resolution before disagreements arise; and formulating rules of safety to prevent harm.

6. *Stay alert to tension and significant changes in talk or behavior.* It's critical to note increased patterns of isolation, alienation, or destructive behavior on

the part of a young person. We too often ignore the signs indicating a significant problem, and the results can be traumatic.

7. *Enable others to shine.* Part of spiritual leadership involves nurturing others as leaders, both youth and adults. This kind of nurture produces amazing results and greatly expands the breadth of ministry. Resist the temptation to gratify your own ego by being the center of attention all the time.

Remember that leaders are also growing in faith. You'll have your own turning points to deal with. When anxieties and difficult challenges arise, they may be beyond you as an individual to handle. It is not, however, beyond God. God provides so many ways of supporting us in our ministry with youth. Your ministry is very important, so don't give up.

Remember, you are not alone!

SECTION two

SECTION TWO

INTRODUCTION

The first section of the book provided the general theological and conceptual framework for a "turning-points" ministry with youth. That section sought to ground you theologically and intellectually as a spiritual leader among youth.

Section Two examines eight types of turning points common among youth. This section centers on how spiritual leaders can enable youth to connect ideas with real-life faith. The following format appears in each chapter:

- **First Glance**—A thought-provoking vignette on some aspect of the theme of the chapter.

- **Heart to Heart**—An introduction and devotional to help the reader "center" so as to engage with each chapter's material at a more personal level.

- **Real Life**—Stories of events and incidents drawn from the lives of youth.

- **Delving Deeper**—A section providing in-depth background information for the theme of the chapter.

- **Tuning In**—Strategies for discovering what is happening in the lives of youth.

- **Twists of Faith**—Suggested activities for helping youth make faith connections and tune into a particular turning point. These activities are intended to spark the imagination, with hopes of inspiring spiritual leaders to develop additional activities focused on the theme of the turning point.

DECISIONS

F irst Glance

Before reading this chapter, reflect on this thought:

We may assume that a young person's destiny—who he or she is and will become—grows primarily out of what happens to that young person or to the circumstances that he or she may face in life. This understanding gains such wide popularity because it expresses a partial truth. Youth, however, deserve to know the full truth. How we *choose to respond* to opportunities or difficulties can be far more important than the difficulties or opportunities themselves.

 Heart to Heart

One of the greatest gifts you can give youth is a faith-filled way to make their own decisions—especially important decisions. The journey from childhood to adulthood produces a tremendous concentration of choices to be made. Talk about relevant ministry! Have you heard this gem of common sense? "Give a person a fish, and you feed her for a day. Teach a person to fish, and you feed her for a lifetime." Well, here's a similar maxim for adults who care about young people: "Tell youth what to do, and you guide them for the moment. Teach youth how to make their own wise decisions, and you guide them for a lifetime." You *can* teach young people skills and ways of approaching choices that will stay with them for years to come, while at the same time you can help them grow closer to God.

Folks will watch how you as a spiritual leader with youth make decisions. People learn even when you may not be intending to teach. This is especially true of young people, who have an awesome capacity to observe and to incorporate new ideas.

One of the fundamental points of this book is that being an adult worker with youth means being a spiritual leader. It's nearly impossible to help others grow in their faith unless our own souls are shaped and replenished by God on a regular basis. So before we talk about how you can help youth face the significant decisions that mark their lives, let's give you as leader a moment to reflect on decision-making in your own spiritual journey.

Begin this time with God by reading each line of the following prayer. As you read a line, think about how you live out the meaning of the line in your own life. Or perhaps think of ways you can make improvements in these areas.

The Prayer of Saint Francis of Assisi

Lord, make me an instrument of thy peace;
where there is hatred, let me sow love;
where there is injury, pardon;
where there is doubt, faith;
where there is despair, hope;
where there is darkness, light;
and where there is sadness, joy.

O Divine Master,
grant that I may not so much seek
to be consoled, as to console;
to be understood, as to understand;
to be loved, as to love;
for it is in giving that we receive,
it is in pardoning that we are pardoned,
and it is in dying that we are born to
    eternal life.

Francis of Assisi, Italy, 13th century

1. Choose an important decision you have made. Think carefully and then write down on a piece of paper the steps you took in deciding what to do in that situation. In what ways did you seek or could you have sought to discern God's guidance in the decision-making process?
2. Read the following Scripture passages and consider the implications for your own life, especially for how you respond to significant decisions.

> Therefore I tell you, do not worry about your life, what you will eat or what you will drink, or about your body, what you will wear. . . . And can any of you by worrying add a single hour to your span of life? . . . But strive first for the kingdom of God and his righteousness, and all these things will be given to you as well." (Matthew 6:25, 27, 33)

> So I say to you, Ask, and it will be given you; search, and you will find; knock, and the door will be opened for you. For everyone who asks receives, and everyone who searches finds, and for everyone who knocks, the door will be opened. (Luke 11:9-10)

> Trust in the LORD with all your heart,
>   and do not rely on your own insight.
> In all your ways acknowledge [God],
>   and [God] will make straight your paths.
>   (Proverbs 3:5-6)

3. Talk with God about the big decisions that you face in your life right now or that someone you care about is wrestling with. Ask God to show you what resources you need to respond faithfully to these circumstances. Listen for God's wisdom; seek God's yearning for this situation.

 Real Life: Stories drawn from the lives of youth

 Work or College

My name is Becky. I grew up going to Sunday school and church most every week. My parents divorced when I was eight, and I went to live with my father. Moving was difficult, but I wanted to be with him. After four years my father remarried. We didn't realize until later that my stepmother is an alcoholic. It has been hard for me to go to her with problems because I don't really know whether I can trust her. This became suddenly even harder when my dad was killed in an industrial accident at work last year. Instead of becoming closer, my stepmother and I have drifted farther apart. It makes me sad, but that's the way it is for now.

I'm beginning my senior year in high school, and I really want to go to college next year. On the other hand, I feel that I should work full-time to pay for living expenses. But my friends are all going to college, and I know that's where I should be too. My youth group leader at church has always encouraged me to make my own decisions, but this time I just didn't know where else to turn. So I asked my youth leader if we could talk. She suggested we meet the next day at the deli across from my school. I explained the difficulty in making a decision about college or full-time work and asked her what she thought I should do. She asked me lots of questions about what I wanted my future to look like and how I could get there from here. Together we looked at all the pros and cons of each decision. It all started to make more sense to me. There was so much to think about.

Then she reminded me that I could ask for God's guidance and presence as I struggle with this decision. She quietly said to me, "Let's pray." So I asked God to help me see what direction was best for my life and to be with me through this stressful time. After sitting silently for several minutes, my youth leader asked me what I was going to do next. I thought about it for a while and then asked her if she would help me with the application forms for college, especially the financial stuff. She assured me she'd be glad to help. After I got home and was talking with a friend on the phone, I realized that my youth leader never did tell me what she thought I should do; instead, she asked me things that helped me see options and possible consequences. She gave me the encouragement to make up my own mind and promised to support me in whatever I decided.

I still don't know how to relate to my stepmother. I guess it's time I finally ask God to help me. In the meantime, I know that my life must move forward and that I have to take those steps myself. But now I know I won't be doing it alone.

Joining the Team

One evening last spring, the phone rang. When I answered, the voice said, "Guess what? I joined the golf team at school!" It took me a moment to recognize the voice of a high school youth I had known for several years through some combined youth-group activities. I was a bit confused because I didn't have any recollection of Jamie ever mentioning playing, or even being interested in, golf.

"So, how did this come about?" I asked. "Oh, the coach stopped me in the lunch room today and invited me to play golf because he didn't have enough players for a team yet. Isn't it great?" she asked excitedly. I didn't know what to say. Jamie is involved in church, sports, and school clubs; she also provides childcare and works part-time. How was she going to add golf to her schedule, and why? So I said, "I didn't know you played golf!" "I've never tried it," Jamie explained, "but the coach says he'll teach me. It can't be that hard, right?" I wanted to tell her all the reasons why I thought this was not a good decision—that it didn't even make sense to me. But I knew that wouldn't be helpful; it might completely crush her enthusiasm. All I could think to say was, "Wow, it sounds like you're really excited. Be sure to let me know how it goes." I hung up the phone just shaking my head and thinking, *She doesn't even know how to play the game. How can she be on the school team?*

About a month later I saw Jamie at a retreat and asked her how she was enjoying playing on the golf team. "Oh, I gave it up," explained Jamie. "I discovered that I don't really like playing golf. But the biggest problem was that I don't have enough time without dropping something else that I like to do. So, I decided to quit. I felt kind of embarrassed to tell my coach, but he was really nice about it—so it worked out fine." I just smiled.

Questions: Did the adults in these stories respond to the young people's questions in ways that helped the youth make thoughtful decisions? If so, how? If not, why not?

Thought: Youth go to those they trust. Seek to intentionally build relationships of trust.

Delving Deeper

How does one go about making a faith-filled decision? We do so much through habit that it's easy to remain oblivious to how we arrive at important choices in our own lives. It is crucial for adult workers with youth to identify their own decision-making process at a conscious level. We cannot guide youth in making decisions when we aren't clear about the process ourselves. Youth need a model—an approach to decision-making they can see clearly and follow easily. It must be simple enough to be remembered.

In talking about a model for making decisions, it is important to remember this caution: Our faith as Christians is not found in a model or in our ability to analyze a situation, or even in knowing clearly what we want. Our faith is in God, the Creator and Sustainer of everything. We are followers of Christ, not ourselves. We believe God is the Source of all wisdom, not us. And we believe God is with us in every decision we face. So as we talk about an approach to making decisions, the question becomes: How do we encourage youth to discern or listen for the yearning of God for their lives and not just their own yearnings—to consider the way of Christ as they make important decisions?

As a way to address this crucial question, we offer a model for faithful decision-making we call the "Decision Circle." It incorporates the various aspects of decision-making into six elements.

The Decision Circle

Our role as adult workers with youth centers on listening to young people with love and helping them travel through the various aspects of making wise decisions. This role plays itself out in two major ways. First, we should look for opportunities to teach the elements of the Decision Circle to the youth as part of our regular youth program. This ensures that when the young people are confronted with making significant decisions, they already have a model to guide them. Remind the group about the model often and use it frequently so that they can come to know it well. Second, when youth come to you for advice about an important decision or opportunity they are facing, the Decision Circle becomes a helpful tool you can use.

We have arranged the elements of the Decision Circle in a particular order. We believe this order makes sense; however, we remain acutely aware that wise decision-making is more of an art than a method that should be followed woodenly. For example, youth sometimes seek our help after they have already made a decision and are dealing with the unwanted consequences of their decision. In such a case it may be better to begin by listening and encouraging them to "assess the impact" of their decision. To stop there, though, fails to adequately address their need; for they come to you looking for hope, wanting to hear again the promise that for every ending there is a new beginning. The youth may not be able to take back some of the repercussions of a decision already made, but he or she can begin to formulate new decisions and choices that will lead in a new direction. This allows the young person to revisit each element of the Decision Circle to once more discern choices that are life-giving.

Some young people may do quite well at one element of decision-making, but skip over or be less skilled at other elements. The youth leader's role is to build on the young people's strengths by guiding them through all the elements of the Decision Circle, even if they don't follow the recommended sequence.

Below is a description of each element of the Decision Circle. The description assumes that the choices are being made by an individual; however, the steps also apply to groups who may need to make decisions together.

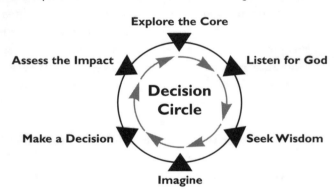

Explore the Core

This element has to do with getting in touch with an identity—a way of being—which enables one to set long-term direction from within rather than being shaped primarily in reaction to external situations. "Explore the Core" also refers to identifying life-giving principles that serve as a consistent, reliable compass when we must choose a way to go. Finally, this element relates to a sense of one's gifts, interests, and calling. (We will cover these in other chapters of the book.)

What do we mean when we say "identity" or "a way of being"? Fundamentally, it means recognizing and cherishing the fact that one is a person made in God's image—a child of God—and responding to life on the basis of that identity. It is imperative to invite youth into an exploration of who they are as children of God, as made in God's image. They need to know that they are children of God and that God is with them (Galatians 3:26-29; Matthew 28:20b). Young people carry within themselves the same creative ability that formed the universe. (See the first and second chapters of Genesis.) They have "response-ability" to shape their own destiny and to bring life to the world. Their lives make a difference, since they can be a reflection of God's love on earth. (See 1 Corinthians 13.)

Youth who know and appreciate their spiritual identity have a much greater capacity to choose wisely than those who lack a sense of identity. Leaders can find ways to help youth ponder who they are in God's eyes so that they can begin to see this identity for themselves and begin to live out of that understanding. For example, a leader may challenge the youth with a question like this: "To be made in God's image means that you are a life-giver. So ask yourself: 'If that's who I am, what is the most life-giving, caring thing I can do in this particular situation?'"

In a similar vein, the Bible talks about the Christian life as a way; that is, living as a Christian is more a way of being than a list of things we do. Let's illustrate the point by reflecting on what is meant when we call someone a truthful person. Being truthful doesn't mean this person tells the truth once or even once in a while. Rather, it means he or she is consistently truthful because telling the truth is a part of his or her *character*. Being truthful represents one dimension of the way of Love—the way of Christ.

The ability to make wise decisions begins long before we encounter a particular choice or a turn in the road. It begins with a commitment to a way of being that will shape all future decisions—an identity that forms the "core" of our existence. To be sure, we still struggle with what is the most loving thing to do in a particular circumstance; but the difference is that the decision we make in any given circumstance is founded on our core identity: a character shaped by the way of Christ. Like Christ, we respond to all circumstances with a sincere desire to love others and to love ourselves. Ignoring these truths leads to an existence of strife and emptiness. Our role as adult workers with youth is not to put guilt on young people, but rather to help them appreciate the joy, meaning, and rich relationships that come to a life based on God's life-giving principles.

Part of the task of leaders is to enable youth to begin to think about who they are and who they want to become so that the youth can create a link between their God-given identity and the decisions and choices they make. Our own experiences of youth teach us that it helps immensely to commit simple phrases to memory. These phrases remind youth to pause and to consider goals and consequences before acting or making a decision. Some of the phrases come from Scripture, and some from writers we admire. Others the youth created themselves. Here are some examples:

- Love one another as I have loved you.   (John 15:12)

- Do justice, love kindness, and walk humbly with your God.
                                               (Micah 6:8, adapted)

- Love God with all your heart, soul, and mind; and love your neighbor as yourself.   (Matthew 22:37, 39, adapted)

- Do to others as you would have them do to you.
                                                      (Matthew 7:12)

- Choose life.

- Make me an instrument of thy peace. (Prayer of Saint Francis)

- Be a light.

- Do good; avoid harm.

- Show me your way.

Listen for God

This element covers a variety of ways in which one can open oneself to God's guidance and can sense God's desire in a situation. We believe that God actually does communicate with those who sincerely seek. "Ask, and it will be given you; search, and you will find . . ." (Matthew 7:7a, b). Divine communication takes on many forms; therefore, youth should be taught and encouraged to listen in a variety of ways too. Inviting God into our lives and pausing to hear God's voice in the midst of competing voices ranks as one of the greatest blessings and efforts for any person of faith.

The following practices have long been effective in aiding people to pause and to hear God's voice: prayer, worship, reading the Bible, silence, guided meditation, audiovisual experiences, readings from inspired authors, singing, individual and group reflection, Holy Communion, preaching, fasting, retreats, service to others, spending time in the natural environment, sensitivity to our own inner feelings—there are many more. Adult leaders should discover opportunities to regularly engage youth in these practices in a meaningful way; they should also involve the youth in shaping and leading such experiences themselves.

Every element of the Decision Circle can be understood as a way of getting in touch with God, of listening for God's voice. As we said earlier, there exists what we call a "sacred space" between what happens and how we choose to respond to what happens. The point of helping youth engage the elements of the Decision Circle is so they may learn to appreciate the importance of sacred space for making wise decisions.

In the sacred space between an event and how a youth chooses to respond to the event, he or she has the opportunity to get in touch with God and to reflect on his or her values, as well as other aspects of making wise decisions. Even if a situation requires a fast response, he or she can still ask for wisdom in some way, such as praying a brief prayer for guidance. The goal for adult workers with youth is to help young people develop a *habit* of seeking wisdom and God's guidance before choosing how to respond to a situation. When youth ignore sacred space, they are controlled by the moment rather than actively shaping it.

Seek Wisdom

This element indicates the need to gather information and to seek the input of trusted advisors. Sometimes we simply need more information before we can choose wisely. For example, if a youth is trying to decide whether or not to join a soccer team, he or she needs to know how much time the sport will take, what the cost is, who else will be affected by the choice to play the game, and so forth. Many poor choices are simply the result of a lack of information.

In addition to gathering data, solid decisions grow out of listening to and receiving input from people we trust and know to be wise. God does speak through other people. Who hasn't at least once experienced the truth expressed in the following passages? "Fools think their own way is right, but the wise listen to advice" (Proverbs 12:15). And "To get wisdom is to love oneself; to keep understanding is to prosper" (Proverbs 19:8).

We do youth a great service when we link them with wise, trustworthy people. It is unrealistic to think that one adult worker with youth can or should serve as the mentor for every youth in his or her care. This means the adult worker can do one of two things. First, he or she can provide opportunities for youth to identify for themselves those people they already trust and consider insightful. It is important that youth understand the difference between finding a person they like to talk to who generally agrees with them, and a person who will be honest with them and who has wisdom to offer. By having a youth identify such trustworthy and wise individuals, and by encouraging the youth regularly to contact these people when he or she faces a difficult choice, adult leaders dramatically increase the likelihood that the youth will act on good advice when the time comes.

> To get wisdom is to love oneself; to keep understanding is to prosper.
> (Proverbs 19:8)

Second, adult leaders can introduce the youth to wise people—both youth and adults—in the congregation and beyond. If the youth comes to know these new people and feels comfortable with them, he or she may seek them out in times of need. This could make a huge difference in the life of a young person. Besides, sometimes the youth just needs to know that someone cares about him or her; this knowledge often provides the strength to make a tough decision.

Imagine

This element represents the process of brainstorming or imagination—of coming up with a variety of possibilities for responding to a situation and of envisioning the potential outcome of each option. Imagination plays a crucial role in bringing new realities into being through imaginative decision-making. Indeed, in a real sense, our decisions and choices represent a primary way of being co-creators with God. Therefore, it's critical to consider what consequences a choice or decision may bring before we act.

Examples of imagination as a spiritual endeavor come both from Scripture and from life experiences. Take the first chapter of Genesis. Verse 3 introduces a phrase that is repeated throughout the chapter: "God said . . ." God spoke a possibility first; then it came into existence. For example, when God said, "Let there be light," light did not exist yet. God first imagined the possibility of light, then created it. In similar fashion, Dr. Martin Luther King, Jr., spoke of a dream for racial justice, motivated by his faith. The dream inspired thousands to work toward a society that did not yet exist and to do what they could to create it.

Adult workers give youth a tremendous advantage when they teach young people how to use imagination in making wise choices. One way to teach decision-making is to have the youth practice imagining the possible conse-quences of a variety of responses to a particular situation. Of each choice, the youth should ask: "If I do this, what do I see as the end result? What would be the potential outcome?" He or she should write down the positive and negative dimensions of each choice. This kind of exercise in imagination provides a young person with better insight into how to choose the most life-giving direction in any circumstance he or she might face. Since the youth does not have to follow through on an option simply because it can be imagined, he or she is able to examine the consequences of a variety of possible choices without actually suffering those consequences.

Make a Decision

This element denotes the act of making a decision and following through on it. Again, youth need to understand that the choices they make have power and will set into motion a series of consequences. It's like throwing a ball. You control the ball until it leaves your hand; after that, it is very difficult, if not impossible, to change its course. Hitting someone with a ball or throwing the ball through a window is probably not what you had in mind. Once that happens, you cannot change it. You might be able to heal the relationship and fix the window, but that will require a lot of extra effort. Knowing exactly where you want the ball to go and becoming proficient at throwing saves you a whole lot of grief and provides a large degree of satisfaction. The same can be said for becoming good at making important decisions.

On the other hand, we don't want youth to become so anxious and worried that they avoid making substantial decisions. (See Matthew 6:25-34.) They need to know that they are loved and supported. The Decision Circle moves youth to consider whether or not a particular decision gives them a sense of peace and helps them move toward God, or whether the decision creates a sense of dis-ease and moves them away from God. However, even the best process cannot guarantee absolute certainty. Therefore, if a decision does not work out, youth need to know that they have a future as well as other options. They need to know that grace, understanding, and forgiveness are available, especially if people are hurt by choices they have made. Youth also need opportunities to celebrate choices that work out well.

Assess the Impact

This element simply means: "Did my decision produce the results I had hoped for or intended? Is the outcome a good one?" If the answer is yes, the youth should celebrate the decision. If the answer is no, the youth should begin the Decision Circle again, leading to new decisions and choices. In the whole decision-making process, adult workers should support the youth as they seek to build their lives.

Tuning In: Ten ways to find out what decisions and choices your youth may face

Consider the ten ways listed below as strategies for discovering the kinds of decisions confronting the youth with whom you are ministering.

- Pay attention to the "side" conversations youth engage in during unstructured time.
- Teach concepts of wise decision-making—the elements of the Decision Circle—and ask the youth to apply these to an actual decision they need to make or have made recently.
- Give youth a list of topics and ask them to circle their interests and concerns. Youth will frequently select topics that reflect issues they are currently dealing with. (See the "List of Topics," pages 157-158.)
- Create programs where youth discuss issues they have selected from the List of Topics.
- Ask youth to write down who they would go to if they need to talk or if they have struggles. They may be willing to give you a confidant's phone number; this information might come in handy for you at some point.
- Directly invite the youth to come to you or to another adult for assistance. The invitation can be as simple as saying: "Hey, if you ever need to talk, give one of us a call."
- Develop trusting relationships with youth.
- Survey the parents occasionally about issues and concerns their children have expressed or concerns that they have about their children.

- Consult with other adults working with your group; exchange knowledge each person has of the situations and issues the youth are facing.
- Watch the youth for changes in behavior that may indicate a problem, crisis, or difficulty. In such cases, you could approach the particular youth directly to find out how you may be of help.

Twists of Faith: Activities that make a faith connection

The activities that follow are intended to spark your creativity as you encourage youth in various settings to grow in faith through the choices and decisions they make. Although these activities are written for use in group settings, many can with slight modification be used by individual young people. Try the activities with your youth group; adapt them; even create your own!

Make an Acrostic (Micah 6:8)

Read Micah 6:8:

> He has told you, O mortal, what is good;
>> and what does the LORD require of you
> but to do justice, and to love kindness,
>> and to walk humbly with your God?

Divide the youth group into groups of three, if possible. Assign each small group one of these words: *Justice, Kindness, Humbly.* Allow the groups fifteen minutes to do the following: (1) Read a definition of their assigned word from a dictionary or a pre-printed sheet of definitions you provide; (2) create an acrostic of the assigned word.

An acrostic begins by writing the letters of the assigned word below one another starting at the top of a page (see example below). Each letter of the assigned word becomes the first letter for a new word, name, or message. If a group's word is *justice,* they choose a word beginning with the letter "J" that helps define, illustrate, or remind them of justice. The second word starts with the letter "U," and so forth. Here is an example of an acrostic using the word *justice.*

> **J** — Joy
> **U** — Understanding
> **S** — Sarah (my friend who stepped in when another kid was being unfairly talked about)
> **T** — Truth
> **I** — Inclusiveness
> **C** — Concern
> **E** — Equity

You can also use words such as *decision* and *wisdom* as catalysts for discussions about wise decisions.

When they are finished with the acrostic, ask each group (or person) to share the definitions and acrostic with the whole group. With the whole group, think about and discuss the following questions:

1. What is God trying to say to me (to us) through Micah 6:8?
2. What one thing could I do, that I am not now doing, "to do justice, and to love kindness, and to walk humbly with your God?" (This discussion may provide an opportunity for the youth to consider making covenants to support and to encourage one another to follow through on the item or items each person names in response to this question.)

Work the Decision Circle

Make enough copies of the Decision Circle diagram (page 72) for each member of the group to have one. Before the group meets, ask six youth to each study the description of one of the six elements of the Decision Circle. As a way to introduce the elements, ask each of the six youth to be ready to explain his or her element to the group.

Invite someone in the group who is willing to do so to describe a real-life decision he or she is dealing with or will need to deal with soon. Then lead the group in a discussion, applying each element of the Decision Circle to the real-life decision. If time allows, repeat the exercise using the real-life decision of another youth.

The purpose of this activity is to teach the youth a specific decision-making process that they can use in their own lives. They can also use the Decision Circle when helping friends and others who face decisions.

Listen for God

This activity involves a time of discussion and quiet meditation. Begin by having the group sing the song "Seek Ye First" (*The United Methodist Hymnal*, 405). Ask two volunteers to read the following passages of Scripture to the group: Matthew 6:33 and Matthew 7:7-8.

In light of the two Scripture passages just read, involve the group in a discussion using the questions below (or you may create your own questions):

1. What good does it do to turn to God when we are trying to make difficult decisions or are struggling with tough issues?
2. What can we expect when we pray for guidance and wisdom? How do you think God might speak to you to help you understand an issue or to give you support when you need it?
3. Where do you see God's presence in your life right now and in the lives of those around you?

Ask each member of the group to identify one decision that he or she is struggling with, or a decision that he or she has recently made. Ask each person to find a place of solitude in the room; however, the group leader should still be able to see each person. Instruct participants to spend ten to fifteen minutes thinking about the decisions they identified earlier and listening for God in silence. (You can extend this time if the group is used to times of silent meditation.) At the conclusion of their time of meditation, encourage participants to write about their feelings, thoughts, and insights.

Reconvene the whole group. Invite participants who are willing to share thoughts and insights they have written down. Remind the youth that they can use this process of meditation and silent listening for God (or a variation of it) at any time. Indeed, there is great value in spending silent time each day listening for God.

Pray together.

Gather Words of Wisdom

Gather enough books containing short readings or quotations so that there is one book for every two members of the group. Talk briefly with the group about the value of listening to the wisdom that others have to offer us, especially in difficult times. Ask each youth to identify at least two people he or she feels are trustworthy and wise and that he or she could turn to in times of trouble. Use your discretion about whether or not to invite the youth to share these names, and the reasons for selecting them, with the group. (It may help you as a youth leader to know who the other support people are in the lives of your youth; however, the youth may choose to share this information with you in private.)

Divide the group into pairs and hand each pair a book of readings or quotations. Allow time for the pairs to browse through the readings and to select one or two readings or quotations they feel are wise and helpful. Ask the pairs to write down the readings or quotations on sheets of paper or on index cards. Afterwards, have each pair post their selections on a bulletin board or on an area on the wall designated "Words of Wisdom."

Reconvene the whole group and read and discuss as many of these readings or quotations as you deem appropriate. (In a camp setting, these readings and quotations could remain on display for the remainder of the camping experience.) Encourage the youth to continue to watch for meaningful writings and to add new readings or quotations to the "Words of Wisdom" area.

RELATIONSHIPS

irst Glance

Before reading this chapter, reflect on this thought:

Faith finds expression in loving relationships.

Truly loving relationships always nurture spiritual growth.

Spiritual growth is the expanding capacity to recognize
and reflect God's presence.

Heart to Heart

[Jesus] said to him, " 'You shall love the Lord your God with all your
heart, and with all your soul, and with all your mind.' This is the greatest and first commandment. And a second is like it: 'You shall love your
neighbor as yourself.' " (Matthew 22:37-39)

Love implies relationships. Jesus invites people by name into relationships as
a long-term method of discipling—teaching others God's way of love. In similar
fashion, relationships are the primary mode of youth ministry. Your leadership
as an adult worker among youth begins by establishing relationships with them.
Before reading any further, complete the following exercise:

1. For the next three to five minutes, list by name the youth you know. Begin
   the list about one third of the way down from the top of a sheet of paper.
   These teenagers may be from your local church; students from other youth
   activities you are associated with; someone who bags the groceries at the
   local supermarket; participants at a camp/retreat event; extended
   family members; or those you know from other settings.

2. Now change the approach slightly. For the next three to
   five minutes, try to think about youth in your community
   you have encountered or heard about, but whose names
   you do not know. They may be groups of youth who hang
   out at the arcade; someone who delivers the paper; friends of
   other youth you know; or a group who regularly play softball
   at the park. Using a few words to indicate who these youth are, generate a list in the space you left blank at the top third of the sheet of paper.

3. In the list of individuals and groups you identified in the top third of the page, put a checkmark next to at least one entry that represents a youth whom you want to get acquainted with.

4. From the group of youth you identified by name, choose those youth that you already have a significant relationship with. Circle their names.

5. Scanning the remaining list of the youth identified by name and the youth identified in the top third of the sheet, place a rectangle around those young people whom you feel deserve special attention because of their circumstances or because you feel led by God to connect more deeply with them.

Prayerfully focus on the youth represented by a checkmark or rectangle. Read the names or descriptions one at a time, pausing to pray for each individually. Open yourself to God's leading about which of these youth with whom God may be calling you as a spiritual leader to establish and to foster a relationship. Write down the names of one to three of these youth whom you will support in new ways. Jot down the names of other caring adults whom you might inspire to consider starting a friendship and a discipling relationship. Close this meditation by thanking God for the caring adults who nurtured you when you were growing up.

 Real Life: Stories drawn from the lives of youth

. . . .

First Love

My girlfriend and I have been dating for three years. We love each other deeply. Our families support our relationship totally. Her parents love me, and my parents, brothers, and sister love her like one of the family. We are both Christians. God is very important to us. We attend church, go to Christian youth rallies, and attend summer camp.

Early in our relationship, we agreed to wait until we were married to have sexual intercourse. I graduate from high school this month, then college starts. We believe that it's important for us to complete our college education before we get married. That's four years from now. Neither of us has ever made love; but lately the topic keeps coming up as we feel more and more drawn to each other. Our relationship has developed over a long period of time—this is definitely not just "recreational sex" we are talking about. We genuinely love each other and want to express that love.

Unlike some of my friends, I can talk with my dad about sex. I told him about the dilemma we were having in deciding what was right. He really listened. After I explained our feelings and conversations, Dad looked me straight in the eye and said, "Son, here's the very best advice I can give you. Do what you think God wants you to do. Seriously consider what is the best and most loving thing to do in the long run. I encourage the two of you to pray, draw insights from your faith, and discuss this very carefully. You are headed for college now. This is the first of many difficult decisions you both will face. I will not be there to make those choices for you." He hugged me and told me that he loved us both.

True Friendship

The stores bulged with Christmas shoppers. The three of us, nearly inseparable, decided to brave the crowds. We paused to enjoy carols being sung by a group of fifth graders. The spirit of the season seemed to be everywhere.

The afternoon at the mall produced an armload of packages, so we set out to make one last stop at our favorite store before calling our parents for a ride home. We meandered down almost every aisle of the store, eventually getting separated from each other by other shoppers. After a while, I noticed that I couldn't spot my friends nearby, so I began to search for them.

I found Carla in the fragrances aisle. I walked toward her, then saw something that shocked me. She was busy stuffing a small bottle of perfume in one of her bags. I couldn't believe my eyes and quickly reasoned that I must be mistaken. I didn't say anything when I reached her because I didn't really know what to say. I truly hoped that I was wrong!

"What's your favorite one?" she asked me, as she continued to peruse the display. I pointed to one that I like, and she reached for it on the shelf. She sprayed some on her wrist and lifted her wrist to her nose. "This is really nice—here, just slip it in your sack," she whispered. "It's so crowded that no one will even notice. The store surely won't miss it!"

Did I hear her right, I wondered? I had never stolen anything before; I wasn't about to start now. "I don't really want it that much," I explained. "Let's just go. It's getting kind of late anyway. But you'd better put that other bottle back before we get in trouble," I urged.

"Oh, you're such a chicken. Do you always have to be perfect?" she asked. I watched her pull the perfume out of her bag. I turned to head toward the store exit. What kind of friend was this who would suggest that I steal from a store? I felt extremely uncomfortable. Our other friend had caught up to us, so we left together.

By the time I arrived home, I wasn't much in the spirit of Christmas. I felt a barrier spring up between Carla and me. We should be giving instead of taking. Didn't she feel this way too?

Should I tell anybody? After all, I did ask her to put it back. It was all so confusing.

Later that evening I went to wrap the gifts to place under the Christmas tree. As I dumped out the bags on my bed, the bottle of perfume I had told Carla to put back tumbled out. I was furious when I realized that she must have slipped it in my bag without my knowing it as we were leaving the store. I had actually walked out of the store with this in my bag.

Clearly, no true friend would do that. Carla had refused to honor my decision not to steal. The days ahead proved painful as I confronted Carla, then returned the perfume to the store. She asked me to forgive her, and, after much thought, I agreed. The foundation of trust so essential to a friendship, however, never fully recovered from the damage. I think of her now and then and wish it could have been different between us.

Questions: What impact did faith in God have in the above two stories? If faith were not a factor, how might things have turned out differently in both cases?
Thought: Relationships spawn some of the most critical turning points in the lives of youth.

 ## Delving Deeper

> Two are better than one, because they have a good reward for their toil. For if they fall, one will lift up the other; but woe to one who is alone and falls and does not have another to help . . . . And though one might prevail against another, two will withstand one. A threefold cord is not quickly broken.   (Ecclesiastes 4:9-10, 12)

The natural desire to belong flowers in full force during adolescence. An unfulfilled need to affiliate with another human being, if too desperate, often leads to unhappiness and pain. It's easy to follow others down unwise paths when one's primary attachments rest with people and groups who lack solid values and decision-making skills. Spiritual leadership among youth means, in part, helping them establish friendships with peers and adult role models, which creates a community of acceptance and belonging.

One of the most critical questions is, How do youth know whether a friendship is good or not? We frequently encourage youth to befriend everyone—not to choose favorites. This is an admirable ideal; but the reality is that youth need to make choices about those people with whom they associate only superficially and those with whom they develop deeper relationships. There are certain behaviors that ought to raise a red flag for any youth trying to sort out the level and depth of his or her friendships and associations. We mention just a few key ones:

- It gets confusing when someone talks about being a friend and says all the right things, but then behaves in a way that makes his or her words a lie. If youth are taught to watch for this kind of discrepancy, they are better able to evaluate the worth of the friendship in light of their own core values.

• One person may use emotional control or power to coerce another person to do something the latter feels uncomfortable doing or feels is wrong. Youth who find themselves in this predicament need to be supported to resist this type of relationship—perhaps even break off the association altogether, depending upon the circumstances.

• When someone insists on pursuing a friendship that is not of mutual interest, there may be reason to question the appropriateness of the one-sided pressure. When this pressure is extreme, one may need to choose to limit involvement with the other person.

Evaluating a relationship may lead a youth to be reconciled to an estranged friend—this can be extremely important. (See Chapter 12, "Family Experiences," for more about reconciliation.) However, evaluating a relationship may lead to situating the relationship at a different, less intimate level, or even choosing to go separate ways.

Most youth instinctively know when it feels right to associate with certain people, just as they usually know when association with someone else may be unwise or even destructive to themselves or others. Our responsibility as adult workers is to give the youth a chance to talk about these feelings and intuitions, and to become more aware of their choices. Sometimes youth just need reassurance that they are making good decisions, or encouragement to consider other options. A good question for the young person to ask is: Do they have the desire or strength to shape a relationship for the good of both parties, or do they need to step back, at least for now?

When we ask youth to identify the most important qualities of a good friend, they usually can make a long and impressive list. They do know the difference between a good friend and an acquaintance, and between a healthy friendship and an unhealthy relationship. The task of adult leaders is to remind the youth to look at their relationships with the qualities of a good friend in mind, and to be alert when something is amiss with a relationship.

Beyond the day-to-day friendships, one of the biggest twists and turns in a teenager's life is the anticipation and experience of dating or of having a romantic interest in someone. While there are excellent resources available on teen sexuality (such as *Let's Be Real: Honest Discussions about Faith and Sexuality* [Abingdon Press, 1998]), one aspect of youth, romance, and dating is worth some discussion here.

Youth often view dating as people getting together to have "fun." While we don't deny that, we believe that dating is also a process of learning how to choose a mate or partner. Of course, we hope that youth are not looking too seriously at finding a mate while still in school! But the practice and exploration of what deeper relationships are all about happen even at this stage as youth ask themselves: What might it be like to spend a lifetime with one other special person as my partner and companion?

Adult workers should not avoid conversations with youth about these issues. Youth, just like adults, want to feel valued in a deeper way, beyond just friendship, so dating often becomes more than entertainment. Many young people are searching for answers to tough questions about relationships, love, dating, and sex; and it is our privilege as adult workers to help them understand how to explore these questions and how these questions relate to their faith and values. Some of the questions youth have should not have to wait! Just ask yourself the following questions: Who usually teaches youth about how to date and how to choose a mate? Who is going to explain that relationships take a great amount of time and effort? Why do we wait until a few months or even weeks before a wedding to begin premarital counseling?

Youth are asking these sorts of questions about romantic involvement: "How do I know if I'm with the right person? How will I know if we're really compatible in the long run? What if I make a mistake?" The following list contains questions—warning signs—to help alert a youth to the possibility that he or she may not be compatible with a partner; the list also contains questions to help youth affirm compatibility. The youth leader should work with his or her youth to add additional warning signs and affirmations.

Warning Signs

- Are there significant things about the other person that you feel must change in order to have a long-term relationship?
- When you have a disagreement, do you end up feeling belittled or put down? Do you question your own self-worth?
- How much do you really know about your partner? Do you know his or her family and friends? Do you ever feel that your partner might be hiding something?
    - Do you tend to feel anxious or worried about whether or not you and your partner will stay together? Does the relationship feel fragile?
        - Do you feel pushed or rushed unduly into a deeper relationship than you are ready for? Are you being asked to do things that make you feel uncomfortable?
    - Does your partner make threats—to break up or to injure you, himself or herself, or others—if you do or don't do specific things? This is tantamount to emotional blackmail.
- Does your partner want to change you significantly?
- Are you bored with the relationship? Your partner may be a very good person, but he or she doesn't seem to keep your interest. Is your interest in the relationship waning?

- Is the timing for the relationship just wrong? Do you foresee the two of you going in different directions at this point or in the foreseeable future?
- Does your partner talk about being "serious" with your relationship, yet continue to date other people at the same time?

Affirmations

- How well do you and your partner solve problems with the relationship? Do you feel cherished, respected, and honored even when you disagree?
- Does your partner value your ambitions? Would he or she help you joyfully to pursue these?
- Do you feel a sense of calm and comfort when you and your partner are together?
- Is your partner a person of faith? Does he or she share your deeply held values and priorities? Does he or she value your time with family and friends? How does your partner relate to people you cherish and respect? What do your family and friends think about your partner?
- Does your partner nurture your soul and your self-esteem? Do you feel stronger within yourself by how your partner treats you?
- Does your partner seem willing to share the mundane and tedious—but necessary—tasks as well as the special times together? How do you get along day after day, not just on special occasions?
- How does your partner spend his or her money? Are these spending habits compatible with your values? Does your partner share what he or she has with others, giving to causes and concerns?
- Is your need for and comfort level with touch and physical interaction compatible with your partner's? For example, it may be difficult if you like hugs and your partner doesn't like physical closeness.
- What are the dominant feelings when you're with your partner?
- Does your partner possess and display the qualities of a good friend?
- Is your partner trustworthy and honest with you?

A key to having a good relationship is our ability to allow another person to see us as we are. This usually means lowering the masks we sometimes hide behind and being open, honest, and perhaps even vulnerable about who we really are. This does not necessarily mean sharing everything about ourselves, but it does mean being honest about the parts of our lives we do choose to share. Another key factor is the need to spend time together, having shared experiences and thoughts. This gives the relationship a foundation on which to build over time.

Patience is a difficult, but important, element as well. If we become overly anxious about the need to develop a new relationship we have begun, we may sometimes scare the other person away, thus producing the opposite of our intention with the relationship.

It is important for adult workers to develop programs in which the youth can explore these key elements of a healthy relationship, as well as the warning signs and the signs of affirmation listed above. Later in the chapter you will find some sample activities to help you do this.

Building Relationships That Last

Examine the following verses of Scripture carefully:

Now concerning love of the brothers and sisters, you do not need to have anyone write to you, for you yourselves have been taught by God to love one another.
(1 Thessalonians 4:9)

Beloved, let us love one another, because love is from God; everyone who loves is born of God and knows God. . . . God's love was revealed among us in this way: God sent his only Son into the world so that we might live through him. . . . Beloved, since God loved us so much, we also ought to love one another. No one has ever seen God; if we love one another, God lives in us, and his love is perfected in us. (1 John 4:7, 9, 11, 12)

Relationships are the foundation of faith. Our relationship with God affects all we say and do in relationship with others. If we truly care about others, we will put aside our selfish ways and work toward others' spiritual growth.

This is not to say our relationship with ourselves is not important. We should try to maintain a healthy balance between self-confidence and self-criticism in order to progress and grow. When we see what is lacking or what needs to be improved in ourselves, we can work toward that improvement. Frequently, leadership arises out of finding this balance between self-confidence and self-criticism. This is a difficult concept for youth to understand. Teens tend to be self-critical and lack the self-confidence to do something about it. They seem to feel justified in putting themselves down. If they are feeling a lack of confidence, they might be afraid to try certain things and will often self-select themselves right out of certain activities that may require, or appear to require, skills, talent, or experience.

Adult workers with youth have a wonderful opportunity in youth and camping programs, local congregations, and other settings to help youth take those positive steps toward trying new things, risking failure in a safe setting, learning skills, and testing and challenging others to accept them. This is one of the greatest gifts you can offer them. It is especially important for youth to develop relationships with adults other than their parents. Because youth are often more open to listening, you may be able to move them toward greater self-expression and self-realization, as well as toward a deeper connection with God. This also means you have a big responsibility to use your time with them in ways that will help them discover who God is, and especially who they are as children of God.

Not all relationships are happy and healthy. Many relationships are torn by distrust, greed, neglect, conflict, and apathy. There are times when even these relationships may be able to change. While we must realize that we cannot change one another, we can change ourselves. By listening, giving, loving, and forgiving when necessary, we may have a profound effect on another person. Equally as important, we may have a profound effect on ourselves, even if the other person does not respond or change. Some relationships will not be salvaged. We can only do what is within our power and ask for God's guidance as we work through difficulties. It is our responsibility to help youth discern the difference between relationships that are healthy and those that are destructive.

> My friends, if anyone is detected in a transgression, you who have received the Spirit should restore such a one in a spirit of gentleness. Take care that you yourselves are not tempted. Bear one another's burdens, and in this way you will fulfill the law of Christ.   (Galatians 6:1-2)

Adult workers can offer youth ways of learning concepts and techniques for conflict resolution, reconciliation, and forgiveness—these are important lifelong skills. If you do not feel competent to teach these ways of learning and these techniques to the youth, you may recruit a specialist in these areas to address the youth group. Excellent resources are available for helping youth learn the skills for developing and maintaining healthy relationships; so use these resources and learn along with the others when the chance arises.

It is vital for each of us to have a certain amount of control over our lives and our relationships. But take note of this caution: Sometimes a person enters the life of a youth and starts making assumptions about the relationship or starts working toward building a certain type of relationship with the youth. This person's desires may or may not match what the youth desires or feels is appropriate. In such a case, it is important for the youth to learn to determine the potential benefits or detriments of the relationship, and then to decide whether or not to pursue the relationship. The youth may choose to enter a relationship with this person, but to do so only at a level at which he feels comfortable and that he deems appropriate. It is wise for youth to be cautious and not to become absorbed—either without realizing what the relationship involves or without actively choosing it—in someone else's plan for a relationship.

Improving Our Relationships

Youth also need experiences that help them understand the concept of loving someone they don't like. Many times, youth base relationships on how they feel about another person. That is all right; however, it doesn't relieve them of the teaching of Christ—that they love others as God has loved them. (See 1 John 1:7.)

Christians believe that human beings are meant to be in relationship with one another, with God, and with all creation. Working with young people gives adult workers wonderful opportunities to practice and carry out this belief and to reflect on who we are as people of God. What are three ways you as an adult worker could *personally* strive to improve the relationships in your life? Write them down.

1. _____
2. _____
3. _____

Faith finds its expression in loving relationships. Truly loving relationships always nurture spiritual growth. Spiritual growth is the expanding capacity to be in tune with and to reflect on the presence of God. As an adult worker with youth, how might you improve your relationship with God? Take time to thank God for being in your life; to invite God into your life; or to ask for forgiveness.

Tuning In: How do we help youth learn more about relationships?

Use the activities below as a way to help youth "tune in" to the struggle and joy of relationships, with God and with others.

- Individually, have the youth write the names of other youth they know well as friends. Then have the youth identify other young people they encounter from time to time whom they do not know well. Have them list people who seem to need a friend or people they would like to get to know better. Divide the group into pairs; ask the members of each pair to tell about one person they know well and one person they barely know. When everyone has finished, assemble the whole group and recall and discuss how they got to know their good friends. Encourage them to introduce themselves and to try to start a friendship with the person they identified as someone they would like to get to know. Give them a week or two to try it and then get back together to talk about how it went.

- Have the youth describe their relationship with God using the following format:

These things about God I feel pretty sure of:

1. _____
2. _____
3. _____
4. _____

These things about God I'm not so sure about:

1. _____
2. _____
3. _____
4. _____

Ask the youth who are willing to share their responses with the group so participants may discover similarities.

- Give the youth a scenario of a relationship that was difficult. Have them explore the possible implications or consequences of various actions; have them roleplay several ways to respond to the relationship.

- Assist youth in evaluating the relationships in their lives by having them complete these open-ended statements:

  _____ (*name*) is one of my closest friends, because _____

  _____ (*name*) is someone I'm struggling with right now, because

  _____

  _____ (*name of person who is not a family member*) is an adult whom I admire, because _____

  I wish I could get to know _____ (*name*) better, because _____

  _____

  Of all my family members, I feel closest to _____ (*name*), because _____

  Add as many additional statements as you would like.

- Ask each member of the youth group to bring a photograph of someone he or she knows and likes (not a family member) and to share with the group why this person is special. This gives the rest of the group a chance to get to know the particular member in a new way and to better understand what he or she admires in people.

- Have each member of the youth group identify someone he or she knows who needs a friend and why. What kind of a friend does this person need? Could the friend possibly be the group member himself or herself, or someone else the group can identify? Pray together for the people identified by the group. Pray that these people may meet someone who will be there for them and care about them.

- Explore with the youth how each person can be a friend to himself or herself. Ask: "Why do you need to be your own friend? What are you already doing to be your own friend?" Have the youth write comments to themselves in their journals or in a letter.

Twists of Faith: Activities that make a faith connection

Use the following activities to help youth connect their faith in God with the relationships they maintain.

Search the Word

Ask each member of the youth group to search the Bible for the word *friends.* Also have the youth search the Scripture for examples of different types of relationships. Have them share the findings with the whole group. (This is an excellent time to teach the youth about how to use a concordance and other Bible study tools.)

Talk About Love

Ask the youth to write answers to the following questions: How do you know what is the best way to love somebody? What *looks* like love but often really isn't love? What are some of the things we do in the name of love that may be more harmful than helpful? What are some examples of the most loving things we can do for those we care about?

Discuss Relationships

Use the following statements and questions to generate discussion about relationships:

1. Name five ways in which you have loved yourself this week.
2. Name five ways in which you have not loved yourself this week.
3. Name a specific behavior you have engaged in or a thought you have entertained this week that was hurtful to you or to someone else.
4. What action can you take that would help you love yourself more?

Have the youth reflect on the following questions as a way to identify times they have practiced love "in disguise":

1. What are some of the ways in which you express yourself that you consider loving but that don't necessarily look or feel like love to others?
2. What are some instances when you have shown love to others when you didn't feel like doing it?
3. What are some instances when you did something for someone anonymously, just because he or she needed it or because it would be a nice thing to do? How did you feel after doing it?

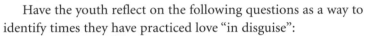

Make a True Friend Outline

Have the youth construct a true friend outline in the following way: Ask one of the youth to lie on his or her back on top of a long sheet of butcher paper. Have someone else trace the person's body outline using a crayon. (Do not use markers, which may damage clothing.) Hang the outline on the wall. Then engage the group in a discussion about what body features are indicative of a true friend. For example: Big ears are good for listening; the heart is the center of compassion and care; strong arms embrace; hands are for helping out in need; and so forth. Next, read Proverbs 15:1-14 to find more examples of a true friend. Choose the most important ones; write these on the true friend outline. Discuss Scripture readings about friends from Proverbs. Close with:

> For it was you who formed my inward parts;
>   you knit me together in my mother's womb.
> I praise you, for I am fearfully and wonderfully made.
>   Wonderful are your works;
> that I know very well.
>
> (Psalm 139:13-14)

PASSAGES TO FREEDOM

irst Glance

Before reading this chapter, reflect on this thought:

Now the Lord is the Spirit, and where the Spirit of the Lord is, there is
freedom. (2 Corinthians 3:17)

Heart to Heart

There are certain freedoms that come with being an adult, a mature person.
What freedoms do you cherish most in your life? Write down ten of these in the
box provided below. Self-determination alone does not guarantee freedom,
though many people believe it does. They equate doing whatever they want to
with liberty.

Think back over your life and the people you've met. Can you remember a
person who did whatever he or she wanted to do, only to discover that his or her
actions led to bondage instead of freedom?

FREEDOMS I CHERISH

1. _____
2. _____
3. _____
4. _____
5. _____
6. _____
7. _____
8. _____
9. _____
10. _____

As a spiritual leader, what does "freedom" mean for your life? To help you respond to this question, read the following passages of Scripture in a spirit of prayer and devotion.

- Now the Lord is the Spirit, and where the Spirit of the Lord is, there is freedom. (2 Corinthians 3:17)

- For you were called to freedom, brothers and sisters; only do not use your freedom as an opportunity for self-indulgence, but through love become slaves to one another. For the whole law is summed up in a single commandment, "You shall love your neighbor as yourself." (Galatians 5:13-14)

- The fruit of the Spirit is love, joy, peace, patience, kindness, generosity, faithfulness, gentleness, and self-control. There is no law against such things. (Galatians 5:22-23)

- As servants of God, live as free people, yet do not use your freedom as a pretext for evil. Honor everyone. Love the family of believers. Fear God. (1 Peter 2:16-17a)

- For people are slaves to whatever masters them. (2 Peter 2:19b)

- Then Jesus said to the Jews who had believed in him, "If you continue in my word, you are truly my disciples; and you will know the truth, and the truth will make you free." (John 8:31-32)

Before writing down any thoughts, spend a few moments in prayer talking with God about your desire for freedom. Then, based on prayerful reflection on these verses of Scripture and on your own experience, write a definition of freedom in the space below. Conclude your time with God by praying for your youth, who are seeking new freedoms as a way to be recognized for growing up.

For me, freedom is _____

_____

 Real Life: Stories drawn from the lives of youth

Freedom and Respon-sibility

During my senior year the track team elected me as one of their captains. What a pleasant surprise! I soon realized that captains had lots of freedoms and privileges. We could leave class early to prepare the team for meets. We chose team warm-up routines. The newspaper and yearbook staff came to us for quotes and information. The coaches consulted us on team morale, strategies to cut down injuries, and so forth. Being a leader brought not only accolades, however; it also presented challenges that I had not expected.

One day after practice, a sprinter came to me wanting to talk. He told me that twenty dollars were missing from his wallet. He knew who had taken it and wanted me to do something because I was a captain of the team. Sure enough, wet footprints on the locker-room floor led from his locker to the locker of one of the premier shot putters in the state. The guy who was being accused was a very likable and popular person with nearly everyone, including me. "What are you going to do?" demanded the distraught teammate. In that moment I understood firsthand that the freedoms that came with being a leader were matched by some very significant responsibilities.

Strange as it may seem, this incident at school—and the question, "What are you going to do?"—launched me onto a powerful spiritual journey. What will the way in which I respond reveal about my character? Teammates looked to me to show the way—I felt tremendous pressure. Stealing threatened the unity of the team. The wisdom of "Thou shalt not steal" seemed undeniable in the face of all the negative repercussions that resulted from that one act. Concepts that I had learned in church suddenly became important in practical ways.

Fortunately, my track coach was a man of faith who listened supportively as I wrestled with what to do. We talked about the meaning of forgiveness, why acting in a caring way is so important within a community of people, how untrustworthy actions can create separation where there was once unity, and a number of other questions. He respected my teary eyes as I contemplated the potential loss of friendships, no matter how I proceeded. He appreciated the inner turmoil about what was best for the team and for the individuals involved. Guidelines for the team had been set early in the season. One of these shared expectations was that anyone caught stealing would be off the team. Did my friend take the money? If so, why? Finally, if we investigated the matter further, would it mean losing an athlete whose participation was critical if the team was to reach the district or perhaps state championship?

My friend admitted stealing the money. He ended up losing his opportunity to be on the team that year, but took it well and learned a great deal. The coach stood by me. I ended up feeling much closer to God somehow. Faith as a way of life suddenly made more sense to me, since it actually had something to do with real life.

The Driver's Education Teacher

In one of his books, Robert Fulghum[1] talks about a retired man who had agreed to be the driver's education teacher for high school students in his local community. The man touched an incredible number of lives. The youth called him Obi Wan (after the great wise man in the Star Wars movies). To be sure, this average man taught young people how to drive a car, but his main purpose was to get them to think about the meaning of their newfound freedom. The teacher engaged the young people in thinking about what they wanted out of life now that they could take off and go just about anywhere. He simply asked questions about what they planned to do and what brought them meaning; then he listened.

Years later the young people of that town still talk about the profound influence that driver's education teacher had on their adult lives. This man turned getting a driver's license into a true rite of passage into adulthood.

Question: What do these two stories reveal to you about how to lead youth toward lives as adults in which they experience true freedom?
Thought: Maintaining freedom sounds easier than it is.

Delving Deeper

Some of the greatest changes or transitions during adolescence involve learning to accept and to negotiate new freedoms. Youth are no longer children, so they do not want to appear dependent on their parents and other adults. Initially, youth tend to lean heavily toward independence, which means autonomy from the control of others. In a way, this tendency should be seen as necessary; we do youth a disservice when we attempt to keep them overly dependent. However, independence, when it means doing whatever we want, is often not freedom at all. When "independence" becomes "self-absorption," people create prisons of isolation for themselves.

As spiritual leaders among youth, we have abundant opportunities to guide youth without controlling them. As youth turn the corner away from dependency and toward independence, will this experience be a twist of faith or a twist of fate? Often young people (and adults, for that matter) believe that simply being able to make choices for oneself equals freedom. Many choices, however, lead not to freedom but to other forms of dependency. As it says in 2 Peter 2:19b, "People are slaves to whatever masters them." We honor our youth when we recognize and celebrate their movement into adulthood. It is a real gift when adult leaders treat youth as mature people and discuss the deeper meaning of their new freedoms.

1 *It Was on Fire When I Lay Down on It,* by Robert Fulghum (Random House, 1992); pp. 71-74.

If we treat our youth like children, we hold them back and fail to enhance their own process of maturing. Over time, as adult leaders begin to relate to youth as equals, they discover that the majority of young people respond by living lives that are increasing in maturity and grace. Adults do not need to tell young people how to act all the time. Youth need the opportunity to reflect for themselves on the meaning of 1 Corinthians 13:11, and its implications for their lives: "When I was a child, I spoke like a child, I thought like a child, I reasoned like a child; when I became an adult, I put an end to childish ways." Adult workers should allow youth to teach themselves by simply inviting young people to honestly ponder the kind of adults they feel called to be. Youth need to name for themselves what are the "childish ways" they seek to abandon.

The path to real freedom takes us beyond dependency. It leads us beyond even independence, because independence fails to incorporate the fundamental reality that life is based on relationships. The whole community of creation is interconnected; nothing can stand alone. In our striving to be "on our own," we must remain acutely cognizant of the spiritual truth that to be truly on our own is the same as being dead. Dependency and extreme independence (or individualism) are childish ways that we put an end to when we become adults within the community.

So what, then, is freedom? Real freedom is not so much self-determination as it is choosing to seek the Spirit. "Now the Lord is the Spirit, and where the Spirit of the Lord is, there is freedom" (2 Corinthians 3:17). It might seem that when we follow a direction other than one we choose ourselves, we give up our freedom. However, because freedom comes from God, when we find the Spirit, we also find freedom.

When we say that freedom goes beyond being independent, we mean that true freedom is the freedom to love—to love other people and the whole community of creation. "For you were called to freedom, brothers and sisters; only do not use your freedom as an opportunity for self-indulgence, but through love become slaves to one another. For the whole law is summed up in a single commandment, 'You shall love your neighbor as yourself'" (Galatians 5:13-14). The dictionary defines an adult as "a mature person," which in spiritual terms means a loving person. Loving means to do what truly nurtures your own soul, the souls of others, and the soul of the whole creation. Purposefully discerning and freely acting on what is most loving is in the long run a mark of maturity.

It is important to encourage youth to consider how easy it is to forfeit the freedoms they have. It's not always easy to remain free. For example, people regularly feel impotent because they give their freedom away—to other people, to organizations, to society, or even to a sense of fate. ("Things happen, and there is nothing I can do about it.") These are the people who live as victims and who blame powers beyond themselves for the outcome of their lives and for their own destructive behavior or failure to act faithfully. Young people need the encouragement to hold onto their freedom in God to live lives of love.

Tuning In: How do we learn more about freedoms youth have and want?

Below are exercises that you as an adult worker can use to become more attuned to the struggle with and yearning for freedom that youth experience.

- *Heighten your own awareness:* Teachable moments hinge on your ability as an adult worker to recognize when youth receive new freedoms; often these are important rites of passage to adulthood. Here are some common examples of new freedoms: receiving a driver's license; going through confirmation; being allowed a later curfew; starting to date; graduating from high school; getting a first job; taking on new leadership roles; becoming a camp counselor or teacher for children; increasing awareness of sexuality and of bodily changes; managing activities of choice unsupervised; being home alone; buying own clothes; assuming new responsibilities within the family; getting involved in social issues; having to pay adult fees for activities and goods; getting ears pierced and wearing makeup; experiencing the first menstruation; choosing a college and taking entrance exams; being selected for teams or performing art groups; and so forth. These transitions provide adult workers with excellent occasions for encouraging youth to develop a life of faith that is real and for reflecting on the meaning of spiritual freedom.

- *Take a freedom ride:* When one of the youth in your group is learning how to drive a car, or when he or she has obtained a driver's license, ask the youth to take you and a friend for a ride. You can drive to some of the young person's favorite places; and you also can talk about the freedom that comes with having a driver's license, as well as about goals and aspirations the youth may have for his or her future as an adult. (Be sure to secure permission from the parents to do this.)

- *I'm ready:* Hand out identical sheets of paper and pencils to everyone in the youth group. Tell the young people to find a private, quiet place where they can write honest responses to the following statements: (1) "A mature person is someone who . . ."; (2) "I wish that adults realized that we youth are (or I am) now mature enough and ready to . . ."; (3) "Before, I used to think or act like a child by . . . , but now I can be trusted with new adult freedoms and responsibilities because . . ." Encourage the youth who are willing to share what they wrote about. Listen carefully to what they say.

- *Survey their family:* Have conversations with or develop a survey for parents of the youth in your group. Ask the parents to talk about how well their son or daughter is maturing. Ask what new freedoms their child has gained this year—both in the home and in other settings—that he or she did not have last year. What new freedoms are they considering granting their son or daughter in the near future? Why? How might you as another caring adult support both the youth and the parents?

Twists of Faith: Activities that make a faith connection

Use the following activities as ways to help youth connect the new freedoms they are experiencing as they mature with their life of faith—to begin to experience the freedom to love.

Prepare for New Freedoms

Have the youth group brainstorm to come up with a list of freedoms or options that adults have and which they as youth are looking forward to having (or which they perhaps already enjoy). You may need to prompt them with some examples to get them started. Have someone record the suggestions on newsprint or dry erase-board. Once all the suggestions have been listed, give each youth a few minutes to review the list by himself or herself. Give each person a pencil and a sheet of paper. Ask the young people to choose from the list two freedoms they most value and to write these on the paper, with room below each freedom for notes. Hand out Bibles or copies of Galatians 5:13-14. Divide the group into pairs. Have each pair read the Scripture passage and discuss its meaning. Following a time of discussion, have each pair reread Galatians 5:13-14; then ask each person to write the following sentence under each of the two freedoms he or she has written down on the sheet of paper: "I will use this new freedom to truly love others by . . ." Ask each person to prayerfully complete the sentence for each of the two freedoms.

Create a Rite-of-Passage Experience

United States society has few true rites of passage for our youth to give communal recognition of their movement from childhood to adulthood. You can create your own rites of passage related to those experiences mentioned above under "Heighten your own awareness" (page 98) or other experiences of youth that mark greater freedom or responsibility. These can include elements of spiritual growth and recognitions of faith. Use your own creativity. Every rite of passage should include three elements: a period of learning and/or preparation; a ceremony or recognized experience marking new maturity; and definite changes in the level of respect, freedom, and responsibility shown toward the young person by the community. These concepts are beautifully illustrated by one Christian family. The children look forward with great anticipation to a weeklong adventure trip somewhere between their twelfth and fourteenth birthdays. Prior to the trip, relatives are sent a separate response form for each youth. The form contains open-ended statements to complete, along with questions that allow the adults to share wisdom they have gleaned in their living and to reflect upon the gifts they see in the young person who is about to embark on an adventure. The youth then study these words of wisdom as part of their preparation and part of the experience. In addition, the young person is given a photographic history of her or his growing up and of the family.

The response sheet sent to the adults includes the following topics:

1. Family Wisdom: I learned the following things from our family that continue to be important to me: _____

_____

2. Someone Special: A person from our family that I wish you had the
chance to get to know or to know better is _____.
Here is a story or some details about that person's life: _____

_____

_____

3. Your Gifts: When I think of the way you are as a person, along with your
skills and talents, these are some of the gifts that I think you have to offer
the world: _____

_____

4. Cherished Values: The qualities I cherish in the people I most admire are

_____

Below is a list of what I consider valuable enough to spend important
time, energy, and resources on: _____

_____

5. Hard Times: When I am having a difficult time in my life, it helps to

_____

I've made some mistakes, and here's what I learned: _____

_____

6. God and Faithful Living: Although I am still on the journey and continue
to discover, these are a few of my experiences and thoughts related to God
and what it means to live as a person of faith: _____

_____

_____

7. I see you maturing and becoming an adult in the following ways:

_____

8. As you move now from being a child toward being a man or a woman, I
especially want to say to you: _____

_____

_____

The youth then do activities that stretch them. They might go white-water raft-
ing, mountain biking, or rock climbing. Or they might do community service, participate in wilderness activities, and so forth. Moments of reflection, heart-to-heart
conversations, and worship experiences the youth lead are also woven into the
experience. Quotes from favorite authors of family members are read and discussed. The week closes with a rites-of-passage ceremony. The young people receive
objects that are reminders of lessons learned. They also receive a family symbol—in
this family's case, a carved stone with an interwoven pattern symbolizing family
unity and the unity of all life in God. The adults are then asked to incorporate the
youth into more adult roles and involvement in the family.

This is just one example of how rites of passage can be created as meaningful
avenues to faith formation and to a closer relationship with God.

ADVENTURES

First Glance

Before reading this chapter, reflect on this thought:

> Journey is more than a metaphor for faith. The Scriptures
> bulge with real-life journeys where people traveled for God
> or encountered the Creator while they were "on the move."

Heart to Heart

> I will lead the blind
> by a road they do not know,
> by paths they have not known
> I will guide them.
> I will turn the darkness before them into light,
> the rough places into level ground.
> These are the things I will do,
> and I will not forsake them.
>
> (Isaiah 42:16)

Recall periods in your life and/or your ministry as an adult worker with
youth when you felt like you were blind, walking on an unclear path. What feelings welled up inside you? Take the next five minutes to share with God your
memories and feelings of those dark, rough places along the way.

In a dictionary, look up the word *forsake*. Write the definition in the box
below, then answer the questions that follow.

F O R S A K E

_____

_____

- What does it mean to you to have the promise that God will not forsake you on your journey?
- How might your life be different were you to truly allow God to guide you? Where might God be leading you next?
- The Bible is jammed with accounts of people who were traveling from place to place. The wise men followed a star into a foreign nation searching for Jesus; Saul (later Paul) met God on the road to Damascus; Jonah reluctantly found himself on a physical and spiritual journey to the city of his enemies; Exodus records the Hebrews' momentous trek to freedom led by Moses; and Ruth pledged to go with Naomi. Search the Bible for significant journeys other than these examples. What happened that made these journeys important? What made them memorable?
- Why do you think adventures serve as such powerful catalysts for encounters with and revelations from God?
- What adventures in your own life, or in the lives of people close to you, triggered significant changes? What was each experience like? What did you learn from these adventures?

> Then when you call upon me and come and pray to me, I will hear you. When you search for me, you will find me; if you seek me with all your heart, I will let you find me, says the LORD, and I will restore your fortunes and gather you from all the nations and all the places where I have driven you, says the LORD, and I will bring you back to the place from which I sent you into exile.
>
> (Jeremiah 29:12-14)

On a sheet of paper, list the highlights of your search for God; these do not need to be in chronological order. Among the most significant places in your search for God, where did you find God? Take time to thank God for these places. You may want to revisit this list from time to time.

 Real Life: Stories drawn from the lives of youth

· ·

Come to the Water

Suttle Lake inherited the frigid cold of the snow-packed peaks of the Cascade Mountains. As we gathered in small groups along the shore of this central Oregon oasis, the stunning beauty began its peaceful healing once again. This lakeside Communion service during Senior High Leadership Camp proved to be life-changing for me.

Several "servants," braving the chill, waded alongside the floating dock. They read to us from the Bible as twilight softened the day. We slowly walked out onto the dock, each in turn, pausing in front of an attendant. We knelt, stretching our hands out over the water. With indescribable tenderness, the person washed my hands. I felt God touch me at that moment. Following Holy Communion, we climbed the hill leading to a tunnel beneath the road that provides safe passage to the camp. Everyone had gone ahead of me, and I became deeply aware that I was alone on the path. As I rounded the corner into the tunnel, two youth beckoned me in silence to grasp their freshly washed hands. In the lingering, dim light, I saw the whole community linked together. I will never forget the feeling of oneness I felt being welcomed into the family of God. We sang and prayed to the God who meets us along the path.

So Little, Yet So Much

Trees lay tossed like pickup sticks across this flattened coastal town. The surreal landscape of twisted metal—snapped and shredded boards that once had been houses—confused the senses. The television images failed to prepare us as we stood amidst the devastation and rubble. We understood, perhaps for the first time, the incredible force called "tornado."

I think all of us felt completely dwarfed by the enormity of the restoration that was needed. What was our small youth group doing here? This situation was way out of our league. Our gung-ho, save-the-world optimism gave way to respectful humility. A tour of the area confirmed the fact that whatever we did would only be a drop in the bucket. Nevertheless, we prayerfully prepared ourselves to pitch in where we could.

The next morning we donned work clothes and gloves and headed for our designated project site to help. To our surprise and delight, the Lopez family greeted us at the foundation of what used to be their home. Timmy, age six, and Tabitha, age eight, became mesmerized by this slightly overwhelming group of teenagers. They rarely took their eyes off of us all morning.

We labored hard for three long days. On the fourth day the Lopez family joined us for lunch. Clearly touched and full of curiosity, they began to ask questions. Why would this group of kids journey all the way across the country to help a family they've never met? What keeps the youth motivated to continue in such heat for long hours? And how do they keep smiling through all of it?

The more vocal youth launched into a recounting of their involvement in the church and their desire to serve others. They shared how they chose to help with the relief effort. Stories began to emerge about intriguing experiences the youth had while traveling across the nation to the relief site. They talked about learning to care for one another and learning to cooperate as a team; they also spoke of other lessons the journey taught them about life.

Finally Tina, one of our quieter and younger youth, stepped forward. With a big smile, she gave each family member a hug; then she summed up in a simple way what was on the hearts of all of the youth: "We love you, and we want you to know that God loves you too. That's why we really came—we loved you before we even met you."

As tears welled up in the parents' eyes, we encircled the whole family. The mother spoke shakily. "We lost almost everything we own and felt like we had so little left. Now we have so much—so much more than we had before. We have new friends; our family is all safe and here together; and when you leave, we'll have a home again. God has surely blessed us and renewed our faith. We will never forget you."

That night, the youth gathered on the lawn at the base of an old lighthouse. We pondered the importance of being a light in the world as we read these verses of Scripture together:

> You are the light of the world. A city built on a hill cannot be hid. No one after lighting a lamp puts it under the bushel basket, but on the lampstand, and it gives light to all in the house. In the same way, let your light shine before others, so that they may see your good works and give glory to your Father in heaven.   (Matthew 5:14-16)

Questions: What made these journeys and adventures so powerful for the people involved? In the second story, in what ways did the youth group receive from the family more than they themselves gave? How can you invite youth into a journey of faith?

Thought: "And when was it that we saw you a stranger and welcomed you, or naked and gave you clothing?" . . . And the king will answer them, "Truly I tell you, just as you did it to one of the least of these who are members of my family, you did it to me." (Matthew 25:38, 40)

Delving Deeper

Adventures supply a plethora of encounters and incidents for youth. Throughout his ministry, Jesus traveled constantly. He used his surroundings and circumstances along the way as poignant object lessons and teachable moments. Youth respond particularly well to this teaching method. Christian precepts go through a metamorphosis from mere rhetoric to practical wisdom when youth see the application to the experiences that mark their own lives.

Experiential learning combines two elements: a teachable moment and a time to process the meaning of the experience. *Teachable moments* refer to those times when young people converge with an object, person, or experience that piques their interest. The potential to learn something new peaks at that moment of intrigue or interest. The longer the interval between the event or experience itself and the opportunity to meditate on its deeper meaning, the more the potential to learn dissipates. The key, then, to supporting a teachable moment is to connect the moment with its spiritual implications as promptly as possible. The way in which this connection is made we call "processing."

Processing means to engage the youth in reflecting on the meaning of their experiences. Teachable moments arise often; adult workers with youth must keep on our toes to recognize these, or they slip by. Noticing that a particular situation gains the youth's attention does not guarantee that the situation will lead to fresh insight. However, when adult workers direct the thinking and dialogue of the youth to what truth about faith or life that a particular circumstance or event might reveal, the incident becomes connected with new understandings. One of the greatest fallacies plaguing families and ministry with youth is the misconception that merely involving teenagers in activities will automatically lead to growth in character and spiritual maturity. Activities are just activities—until we introduce spiritual reflection on the meaning of these activities.

Some people refer to the concept of experiential learning we have been exploring in these paragraphs as "action-reflection." *Action* spans the spectrum from the plain act of observation to the challenge of cooperating with others in shared projects. *Reflection* refers to the process of examining the experience to discover insights and implications for growing in faith and in awareness of God's presence. Scripture is filled with thought-provoking instances of experiential learning, coupling action and reflection in insightful ways. Consider the following passages from the New Testament:

> He sat down opposite the treasury, and watched the crowd putting money into the treasury. Many rich people put in large sums. A poor widow came and put in two small copper coins, which are worth a penny. Then he called his disciples and said to them, "Truly I tell you, this poor widow has put in more than all those who are contributing to the treasury. For all of them have contributed out of their abundance; but she out of her poverty has put in everything she had, all she had to live on." (Mark 12:41-44)

In the above verse, how did Jesus use what he observed in this occurrence to spark a new perspective among the disciples?

> As he walked by the Sea of Galilee, he saw two brothers, Simon, who is called Peter, and Andrew his brother, casting a net into the sea—for they were fishermen. And he said to them, "Follow me, and I will make you fish for people." (Matthew 4:18-19)

In the above verse, how did Jesus use an activity that already interested these men (fishing) to introduce a new spiritual journey?

> Then they came to Capernaum; and when he was in the house he asked them, "What were you arguing about on the way?" But they were silent, for on the way they had argued with one another who was the greatest. He sat down, called the

twelve, and said to them, "Whoever wants to be first must be last of all and servant of all." Then he took a little child and put it among them; and taking it in his arms, he said to them, "Whoever welcomes one such child in my name welcomes me, and whoever welcomes me welcomes not me but the one who sent me."

(Mark 9:33-37)

Then he poured water into a basin and began to wash the disciples' feet and to wipe them with the towel that was tied around him. He came to Simon Peter, who said to him, "Lord, are you going to wash my feet?" Jesus answered, "You do not know now what I am doing, but later you will understand." Peter said to him, "You will never wash my feet." Jesus answered, "Unless I wash you, you have no share with me . . ." After he had washed their feet, had put on his robe, and had returned to the table, he said to them, "Do you know what I have done to you?"

(John 13:5-8, 12)

How did Jesus use teachable moments in the two Scripture passages above to inculcate a spiritual truth? (Interestingly, even conflict provides teachable moments.)

Often teachable moments occur naturally; but like Jesus, adult workers can create activities for youth to experience and then to reflect upon or process.

Artful questions and enticing thoughts represent the mainstay of processing an adventure or experience. When a teachable moment arises, or when you create one, formulate open-ended questions that require more than a yes or no response; you want the young people to examine their own inner feelings and ideas. Teenagers can sometimes amaze adults with their ability to connect these feelings and ideas with spiritual wisdom. Your questions should move the youth in the direction of greater wisdom. We hope that eventually self-reflection about their lives or the things they observe will become a habit with youth to the extent that they won't need to depend on the guidance of adults. However, sometimes a concept or experience is new to the youth, and they lack the resources to understand and to express its meaning. In such a case, it is important for adult workers to bring their own experience and insight to bear on the issue—this adds breadth to the young people's task of processing the spiritual meaning of the experience. Generally speaking, it is better for adult workers to help the youth find their own responses to an event or situation before the adults share their own insights, because when a youth recognizes a truth for him or herself, it is often more powerful than being told what an event or concept might mean.

Many other valuable techniques are available to help youth reflect on the teachable moments in their lives. For example, the youth can take photographs of an event or experience that is meaningful to them, if the event or experience lends itself to it. They can also write their reflections in a journal or a letter to themselves or to a friend; or they can share their feelings and insights in small groups or through art or drama. As an adult worker, be creative and use a variety of ways to get the youth to reflect on their experiences. This keeps the youth's task of processing their experience more lively and interesting and also enhances learning and spiritual growth.

Adventures have a well-deserved reputation for making pivotal spiritual experiences possible. In large measure, this has to do with the fact that adventures have the unique characteristics that produce perfect conditions for experiential learning to take place. That is, adventures free the young people from their normal routine; actively involve them with engaging new environments and people; and concentrate their attention on spiritual growth.

Routine activities—such as going to school, doing chores, maintaining friendships, watching television, engaging in sports—often distract youth from growing spiritually.

Adventures create an entirely different rhythm, disrupting— sometimes even eliminating—normal patterns of behavior. Such an alternative rhythm allows a person to direct his or her attention to the events and circumstances of daily life in fresh and spiritually heightened ways. Allowing the unique rhythm of an adventure to refocus attention on the link between faith and daily living often transforms lives, sometimes within a few days or weeks. Some youth allude to this when they remark that a single week of camp or several weekend retreats compares to an entire year's worth of interaction at church school. Adventures will never replace the weekly practices, but what an enhancement they can be for spiritual growth!

Adventures nearly always require physical action. It is hard to remain dispassionate when climbing your way up a hundred-foot cliff or balaying another climber who entrusts her or his life and well-being to you. Talking about feeding the hungry cannot possibly teach what actually preparing, serving, and getting to know people who are poor does. Leading a day-camp experience for prisoners and their families accomplishes more than merely reading "I was in prison and you visited me" (Matthew 25:36b) a hundred times. Traveling and working twenty-four hours a day with a group of friends (or, heretofore, strangers) makes it difficult to hide superficiality. Living together like this calls us to apply the principles of Christian community at new levels at times when doing so may not be easy. Youth regularly learn best by doing that which takes them beyond the norm. This may be uncomfortable for the youth, or it may be exciting; in either case, it stretches them both personally and spiritually. Such challenges to move beyond themselves create a great deal of food for thought for young people.

Properly managing risk so as to ensure the health and well-being of youth is a crucial task for adult workers. Youth leaders should do an activity only with the help of properly trained leaders and using proper equipment. They should never cut corners when it comes to the young people's safety. Both the youth and their parents are placing their trust in the adult workers, and are holding these adults accountable for the safety of all involved. The American Camping Association can connect youth workers with people in their local areas who can teach about risk-management procedures (telephone: 765-342-8456); or leaders with youth can purchase books on the topic from the Association's bookstore (telephone: 800-428-CAMP).

Finally, well-conceived adventures expose youth to God. By praying, studying, and preparing for a mission trip, young people may begin to experience humility and genuine compassion. By encountering a person with a vibrant faith in God, a young person's own faith may be bolstered; or the experience may expose a misconception the youth has had about the life of faith. By reaching out in compassion to people in need, the youth may feel the presence of the Holy Spirit within them or may gain a new sense of their own worth as children of God. They may learn that they receive much more than they give. The point is that when an adventure is genuinely dedicated to God, God usually shows up!

Adult workers need to find ways to integrate the "extraordinary" adventures into the ordinary routine of the youth's daily existence; otherwise, these pivotal experiences threaten to become isolated and disconnected from their day-to-day lives. Adult workers need to help congregation members and parents understand how significant an adventure or journey is to the youth and help the members and parents honor the changes that have taken place in the youth as a consequence of the experience. It's a demoralizing shock for young people to come home to the "status quo" with no recognition or appreciation of the significance of what has happened to them. If the learning gained through the adventure is not linked with daily life back home, it will be hard to maintain what was gained.

In closing, tantalize your youth with the possibilities of being "on the move" with and for God. "Then I heard the voice of the LORD saying, 'Whom shall I send, and who will go for us?' And I said, 'Here am I; send me!' " (Isaiah 6:8).

Tuning In: Ways to learn more about new adventures

The activities and suggestions below help adult workers "tune in" to creative ways to engage youth in adventures that may transform their lives and deepen their faith experience.

- *Ask other leaders:* One of the best resources for discovering how to involve youth in powerful experiences and activities is to ask other youth leaders, particularly leaders who have led youth mission trips or service projects; directed camps and retreats; went on group challenge-courses; conducted workshops; lived in other cultures and/or countries; or worshiped with people of other religions. By drawing on their experience and knowl-edge, these leaders can tell you which adventures have worked well and what these have meant to them and to the youth who participated. Usually they can also provide you with the names and phone numbers of people or organizations to contact for more information.

  - *Ask the youth:* Have the youth write down the names of places they have visited during a trip that was particularly intriguing. Or ask them to jot down activities they have engaged in that were exciting and adventurous; they could include activities mentioned by friends who were excited about a particular experience. Use this information in formulating adventures for your youth that can be used as a platform for Christian formation.

- *Plan a highway-signs activity:* Fasten a sheet of newsprint on the wall where everyone has access to write on it. Provide everyone in the youth group with markers. Ask participants to take turns writing on the newsprint words and phrases they can remember from highway signs they've seen. These words and phrases may include: detour, curves ahead, stop, caution, workers ahead, speed, under construction, dead end, one way, congestion, keep in the right lane except when passing, animal crossing, two-lane road ahead, slow, narrows to one lane, no passing, yield, and be prepared to stop. Give each person a sheet of paper and a pencil. Ask participants to draw a timeline of their lives— from birth to the present—in the form of a journey, using the road signs the group has written on the newsprint as ways to describe specific times on their life's journey. Offer the youth a chance to share some of the highlights of their journeys. Next, lead the group in a discussion of the questions below. Afterwards, close the time together with prayer, asking that you and the youth may see the signs of God's working in your lives more clearly.

    1. Can you think of a time when your life's journey seemed to take a "detour"?
    2. Have there been times when you've had to proceed with "caution"?
    3. When have you felt like your life was "under construction," or that you have been building or rebuilding parts of your life?
    4. In what ways could your life's journey be made easier by others? What would be different if you were to journey together with others? Would you have more support? Would you feel less lonely?
    5. Where have you experienced or sensed God along the journey of your life?

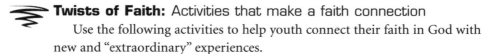

Twists of Faith: Activities that make a faith connection

Use the following activities to help youth connect their faith in God with new and "extraordinary" experiences.

Stage Journey Dramas

Get enough Bibles for everyone in the group to use one. Ask the youth to find several stories in the Bible of people who are traveling or who are in the midst of some adventure. Divide the youth into small groups. In the small groups, have each person share the story he or she has found that could best teach something valuable about God and about the life of faith. After each person has proposed a story, each small group should choose from among the stories one story to dramatize. If the story does not have enough "people" parts for every member of the group, some members can play "objects" to create the scene. Ask each small group to practice its drama, then to present it to the whole group. Have the whole group discuss the main points of these dramatized stories and how insights from each drama apply to their lives today.

Sign up for Camp or Go on a Retreat

Ask your pastor how to contact The United Methodist conference or judicatory office in your area, so that you can call and get the latest camping brochure. Conferences and judicatories also sponsor youth rallies and retreats; you can also plan your own retreat or camping experiences. Call InfoServ (800-251-8140) for information and telephone numbers related to United Methodist camps and retreats in your region. This service also can tell you how to reach local camp/retreat centers in your area. In addition, the following web pages from the General Board of Discipleship's web site will aid you:

http://www.gbod.org/camping/default.html
http://www.gbod.org/youth/default.html

Fulfill the Scripture

Study the following passage of Scripture with the youth group:

When [Jesus] came to Nazareth, where he had been brought up, he went to the synagogue on the sabbath day, as was his custom. He stood up to read, and the scroll of the prophet Isaiah was given to him. He unrolled the scroll and found the place where it was written:
"The Spirit of the Lord is upon me,
    because he has anointed me to bring good news to the poor.
He has sent me to proclaim release to the captives
    and recovery of sight to the blind, to let the oppressed go free,
to proclaim the year of the Lord's favor."
And he rolled up the scroll, gave it back to the attendant, and sat down. The eyes of all in the synagogue were fixed on him. Then he began to say to them, "Today this scripture has been fulfilled in your hearing."
(Luke 4:16-21)

Ask the youth to brainstorm about ways they might join Jesus in bringing good news to the poor, proclaiming release to captives and recovery of sight to the blind, letting the oppressed go free, and proclaiming the year of the Lord's favor. You can help by researching opportunities for service or mission work that involve these biblical themes. Lead the youth group in pursuing such an opportunity as a way of concretely participating in the vision of Luke 4:16-21. Process the experience afterwards.

Take the Youth on a Group Challenge/Ropes Course

Find a local challenge course that is properly built, inspected, and administered. Normally camps or retreat centers, public schools, colleges, and park and recreation programs are the main settings for such courses. If these institutions do not operate a challenge course themselves, they may be able to tell you where to find one. Ropes courses provide awesome dynamics for building trust and cooperation among the youth. Find a facilitator who would be willing to lead the youth in times of reflection on this adventure, helping them make connections between their experiences and Scripture and assessing ways to grow spiritually. An excellent resource for learning how to reflect on adventure experiences with faith in mind is *Go for It: 25 Faith-Building Adventures for Groups,* by Walt Marcum. (See "For Further Reading" on page 155 for information on this and other resources.)

LOSS, CRISIS, & RECOVERY

First Glance

Before reading this chapter, reflect on this thought:

> God is our refuge and strength,
> a very present help in trouble.
> (Psalm 46:1)

Heart to Heart

It's a natural tendency to resist or to run from what is difficult and painful. The "fight or flight" instinct still kicks in as a frontline defense whenever we face potential or real danger—the threat of physical or emotional hurt. Times of crisis and loss have such a huge impact on us precisely because of the uncertainty and intense emotions they elicit. Experiences of crisis and loss shake us to the core of our being. They strip away unimportant issues and leave us contemplating the final meaning of our lives and assessing what is truly valuable. In one way or another, all loss and crisis remind us of our own mortality or the mortality of those we love. This can be very uncomfortable, very distressing.

In this chapter we invite you who are spiritual leaders among youth to do something counter-intuitive: We want you to learn to welcome loss and crisis. We are not suggesting that you wish for or cause unnecessary loss or crisis, but that you learn not to fear and not to avoid these times. Hardship has a way of drawing people to the essentials of life, including the essential reality of God. By learning to welcome loss and crisis, you will not shy away when youth or their families enter dark times and look to you for spiritual help. Instead, you will be a conduit of God's presence, allowing God to move through you as you listen and seek to understand what support to offer.

Some situations of crisis and loss in the lives of youth can be very painful. In order to get in touch with this pain, we would like you to revisit a significant crisis or an experience of loss in your own life. We realize that doing this is challenging and potentially painful, because to remember the event means reliving it at some level. If trying to remember a particular experience of crisis or loss is too overwhelming for you, we encourage you to choose another event to reflect on, or to invite a trusted friend to join you for this "remembering" process.

To begin the process of remembering a crisis or loss you have experienced, find a quiet place where you can reflect undisturbed. Allow the following questions to guide your thinking as you remember the event. (By the way, these same questions can be adapted to help youth and their families "process" an experience of crisis or loss they are going through.)

1. What happened to cause the crisis or loss?
2. Who else was involved? How was this person (or people) involved?
3. At the time of the crisis or loss, were other aspects of your life out of balance, or were you dealing with other losses as well? If so, how did these other factors affect the crisis or loss you are now recalling?
4. What additional factors and what other people contributed to the overall hardship?
5. What were your honest thoughts and feelings about the experience of crisis or loss at the time it occurred?
6. Who or what provided you with support and hope during your struggle?
7. Did you mull over the possibility of harming yourself or someone else?
8. Were you receiving professional care of some kind at the time?
9. At the time, what did you want to say to God about the crisis or loss?
10. Romans 8:28a says, "We know that all things work together for good for those who love God." Apparently, even bad situations cannot overpower God's desire to bring us good. As you look back on the experience of crisis or loss you are recalling, what good, if any, do you believe came out of your hardship?

Read Mark 14:32-43. Do you think this was a crisis moment for Jesus? Why or why not? Spend time talking with God about the times of crisis and loss you have experienced in your own life. Ask God to help you understand your role in helping youth and their families gain a deeper trust in God when they find themselves in difficult times.

Real Life: Stories drawn from the lives of youth

· ·

My
Aunt

Things just started stacking up. My parents decided to move to take advantage of a new job opportunity. Maybe it was good for them, but it turned out to be a mess for me. I pretty much sat on the bench for my entire senior year of football; no one really knew me, and the starters had already been chosen. I was doubly dismayed by widespread use of drugs and alcohol in the new school. I felt completely out of place and lonely.

My younger sister was finding it hard too. She wanted to hang around me for support. I didn't mind much, but it felt like a big responsibility in a new town that was a lot rougher than the town we had known before.

Finally I met a girl, and things seemed to be looking up. We went out on a date a couple of times, but I didn't want to get as serious as she did. I broke off the relationship because I knew that it was not going to work out. Shortly thereafter, people at school and in the community started to treat me coldly. I couldn't figure out why. Eventually a friend came up to me. "Did you try to rape Mary? That's what she is saying."

I could not believe Mary would spread a rumor that awful just because I did not want to date her. If she was trying to make my life a disaster, it worked. As you can imagine, a lot of people tended not to believe me when I claimed that Mary was lying. I was new to town. They didn't know that I would never do anything like that. I was devastated. I was the victim, but people were ostracizing me. My life was falling apart.

During this same year and a half, my parents were struggling with their marriage. They had enough problems of their own. I didn't know who to talk with about all this. Unfortunately, the pastor of my church treated me as if the accusations were true. He did nothing but add salt to my wounds. I had no one to talk to— then I remembered.

I turned to the one adult whom I felt would understand: my aunt. In the past, she spent a lot of time with me, taking me places and doing things with me; so I felt I could trust her. I sat down with a tape recorder and let it all pour out—all the anger, all the pain. Since my aunt lived hundreds of miles away, I put the tape in an envelope and mailed it to her.

Later that week, my aunt called the house to say that she was coming to visit the family. She drove for hours, and I knew she did it mostly for me. She arranged for some one-on-one time to talk. We sat and listened to the tape again together. We discussed it all. She never judged me. She even gave me a book that helped me comprehend what my parents were going through. What I learned helped me immensely with my own marriage later.

Her visit, her nonjudgmental support, and the fact that she continued to invest time in me helped keep me open to God. Without her and a few other compassionate adults, I might have written God off altogether. In college, I came to a deep faith in God, which has blessed my life.

What to Do?

Just a few days ago, the pastor told me something about a young man in my youth group that caused me great concern. I don't want to cause him and his family a lot of grief, but he could be getting himself into some major problems. Based on past experiences, his parents will cringe at anything that might look like criticism of their son, even if the criticism is offered in love. They threatened to leave the church before over issues unrelated to the youth group. It would frustrate the church staff and some members if this family got miffed and left; after all, they are one of the largest financial contributors to the congregation's budget.

Larry could really screw up his life, though. Our pastor works with street kids in the inner city. He saw Larry one night drive up to a known heroin dealer in a dangerous part of town and buy drugs. The pastor identified Larry without hesitation—he recognized Larry's car and saw Larry close up. He knows Larry well, so a mistake seems highly unlikely.

Am I going to create a crisis here or help prevent one by reporting this incident to Larry's family? Is there any way to address this situation without alienating someone?

Questions: What insights or reflections do these two real-life situations elicit? How can an adult leader with youth reflect God's love and presence among young people going through hard times?

Thought: "Nothing can separate us from the love of God." (See Romans 8:38-39.)

Delving Deeper

As adult workers who are also spiritual leaders, what is our ministry when youth encounter loss or crisis? The answer takes shape from a consideration of the nature of loss and crisis itself; it also has to do with remembering our unique purpose as leaders in Christian youth ministry.

Dealing With Loss

Loss represents death at some level; what once existed no longer remains. Loss might involve the end of a relationship, a lost opportunity, or a dream for the future that now appears unlikely. Even loss of face or status with peers can devastate. Loss takes a thousand forms. In each case, the future seems darker, less promising. At its worst, life appears to be a dead end.

The confusion accompanying an experience of loss might be compared to having the lights go out while exploring a cave. All of a sudden, the situation changes dramatically. The normal points of reference seem to disappear, making it extremely hard to find your way back to normalcy. Loneliness and anxiety often set in. You are no longer confident about which way to go. You grope along, straining to see the tiniest shaft of light that reveals a way out. An adventure now becomes a trial. As your energy begins to wane, you may wonder if you will ever emerge to see a brighter day.

What youth and their families need in situations like these is light; that is, they need people who will reflect light into the dark places so they can find their way out of a situation of intense struggle. Even small acts of love and hope can pierce the bleakness of people's pain. People need to hear that a worthwhile future awaits them. Adult spiritual leaders need to respect the complexity of the struggle these people face; therefore, they must go beyond reciting religious sayings to embodying the love and hope of God. As a spiritual leader, hang in there and reflect the light of God in word and in deed, until those in the midst of loss see God's light. Listening intently and carefully is crucial; only in doing so can you know where and how to best offer glimpses of hope.

Well-intended leaders sometimes emit darkness rather than light in trying to help people during times of loss. The following approaches are often more hurtful than helpful. Indeed, in some cases these approaches nearly destroyed people's faith in God rather than enhancing it. (Unfortunately, much of this came in the guise of religion.)

- Some leaders become so emotionally involved in the suffering of people they are trying to help that they themselves become distraught; this merely adds to the problem. It's not much help to have someone walk into the cave with me and bring no light, then remind me repeatedly that I am in darkness. I feel like I now have the burden of helping myself and this person too.

- Some leaders chastise youth for getting themselves into a situation of loss at all; this does not help. The fact that my behavior is largely to blame for my current dilemma is an important lesson I need to learn; however, the first thing I need to know is that you are more interested in helping me find my way out of the dilemma than in telling me what I did wrong.

- Some leaders seem to imply that the cause for the young person's experience of loss has to do with unconfessed sin in the youth's life. This leads one to wonder whether God cares more about rules than about the one who suffers. The emotional pain such a view can inflict is severe. It often impels the person into a state in which he or she tries to recall and confess every last sin, leaving the person worn out. Sometimes unthinking leaders suggest to someone who is facing the worst possible loss—death—that somehow his or her dying is connected with God's desire to teach him or her something. The logic of this position—namely, that to teach your child a lesson you must injure him or her severely—is tantamount to child abuse. Adult leaders need to think carefully and clearly about the implications of what they are saying.

- Some leaders suggest to young people experiencing loss that if they just had more faith in God, their problems would end. The difficulty with such reasoning is obvious: Many young people finding themselves in the midst of loss are deeply devoted to God and are praying earnestly for a way out. Yet the experience of loss remains. So they ask an appropriate, albeit depressing, question: *Is God refusing to help me simply because I don't know how to conjure up more faith?*

Coping With Crisis

Let's move now from the experience of loss to that of crisis. *Crisis* refers to a change in a person's life so radical that it undermines the person's sense of grounding and stability. An experience of loss may produce a crisis, but so can other situations. For example, getting a job or a part in a play that you really want might move you into a whole new arena, both unfamiliar and disorienting. In such a new setting, your normal supports are absent. Take another scenario: In your job, you handle several basic responsibilities, but the difficulties you encounter are usually minor. But then a barrage of minor difficulties hits you all at the same time, throwing you completely off balance. In the midst of the confusion, you begin to realize that life as you live it lacks the meaning it once held. So you feel compelled to make a change. All of a sudden you find yourself in a crisis.

Imagine the difference between walking on solid ground and having that ground drop away, leaving you on a four-inch-wide balance beam—being in the midst of a crisis sometimes feels just like this. Even accomplishing simple tasks like walking causes stress. Sometimes adult leaders shake their heads in frustration when youth seem to be overly dramatic in describing a stressful situation. To adults, what youth describe may appear to be much ado about nothing. Youth behave in ways that strike adult leaders as a complete overreaction to a situation. When this happens, though, adult workers should pay attention. Overreacting to a relatively minor issue could indicate that the ground may be shaky in other areas of the young person's life, and that he or she is struggling to adapt and cope.

A valuable concept for all adults who work with youth to remember is this: It is the young person going through a stressful situation who determines whether the situation is a crisis or not—not the adult worker. Adult leaders must be careful not to belittle a young person for finding it difficult to handle predicaments that are a breeze for the leader or for other youth. Not everyone has a natural talent to walk a balance beam! When a junior high romance ends, adults may smile, knowing that the breakup was inevitable. But adults must simultaneously respect the fact that the end of this relationship truly strikes the young person as a tragedy. It is a very real crisis for that youth.

Ministering in the Midst of Loss and Crisis

How can our ministry as adult workers effectively boost the recovery of young people who are experiencing loss or crisis? Here are a few suggestions to keep in mind.

- *See the losses behind the loss.* There is never just a single loss; a loss always triggers or involves other areas of loss. For example, when a young person gets cut from an athletic team, the disappointment involves more than the fact that his or her name does not appear on the team roster. The youth loses time with friends; skills he or she had hoped to gain; the positive regard of other students; a worthwhile activity to occupy his or her time; and so forth.

- *Let them feel.* Expressing feelings represents a form of honesty, for it exposes what's going on inside the young person's heart and mind. Honestly expressing his or her feelings is a crucial first step on the way to healing. When adult workers reject a youth's feelings, the young person tends to hide the woundedness. This makes it difficult to heal the wound. Adult workers need to realize that feelings are neither right nor wrong; however, how leaders respond to feelings can be positive or can cause problems. Adult spiritual leaders need to recognize this distinction and need to allow youth to share their feelings without feeling judged. When this happens, youth will trust adult workers to assist in their recovery.

- *Do not walk the "balance beam" for them.* Walk alongside the young person experiencing loss or crisis, and remain present to offer support at the level the youth needs in order to "keep balance." Sometimes the support required is massive; at other times, it only takes a finger for someone to maintain his or her equilibrium. When adult leaders try to assist too much, they get in the young person's way and can trip them up. Adults should try to expand the youth's own ability to cope and to develop bases of support, the goal being that the youth will eventually master walking the balance beam for himself or herself. The youth may learn to excel at handling crises, which will reduce the number of incidents that create trauma. This confidence produces a sense of peace previously unknown to many youth.

- *Relay the message of unconditional love.* Make sure the person knows that God and you as an adult leader love him or her dearly and without ceasing. The young person needs to know that you are looking out for his or her best interest at all times. Provide empathy through in-depth listening that seeks to understand and, through cheering him or her on, to help that young person succeed.

- *Ride the "waves."* Be aware that recovery occurs in waves. That is, you will find that the young person in the midst of loss or crisis copes fine one minute, only to go to pieces the next minute. When something happens to remind the young person of the loss or crisis, it washes over him or her again. Tell the youth that such experiences are normal. As an adult worker, prepare yourself to support the young person during this time of emotional upheaval. Over time the "waves" will be farther and farther apart. But it takes time, so expect the young person's behavior to be inconsistent for a while.

- *Assure them of the light at the end of the tunnel.* Youth and their families long to know that a new beginning awaits them. God brings resurrection to every ending. But we first have to experience the ending; then the beginning comes.

- *Gather additional information.* Adult workers can tap alternate sources such as family and friends, when appropriate, for a more thorough understanding of the situation a youth is experiencing; this increases the leader's wisdom and ability to be helpful during a crisis or loss. There is often more going on than the perspective of the youth alone may reveal.

- *Slowly introduce new concepts and solid possibilities for the teenager to consider.* It's a huge challenge for a young person walking the balance beam of a crisis or loss to juggle new ideas and tasks. It is easy to make rash moves that can destabilize the situation further.

- *Connect them with other support systems.* Sometimes the crisis or loss a youth is experiencing warrants professional help. Be ready to refer if the situation calls for it. Avoid promising confidentiality prematurely; this can land you as adult worker in a real dilemma. (See Chapter 5, "It's Beyond Me!" for a discussion of the limits of confidentiality.)

- *Support a "faith-full" recovery plan.* Eventually the youth experiencing a loss or crisis will need to discern what to do next. To assist him or her in making the kinds of decisions that will aid in recovery, introduce the youth to the Decision Circle model outlined in Chapter 6, "Decisions" (pages 67–80).

For a more detailed treatment of how to help in a crisis or loss, we recommend Rich Van Pelt's book, *Intensive Care: Helping Teenagers in Crisis.* Since this book is out of print, you might check your public library or your church library.

> I will show you what someone is like who comes to me, hears my words, and acts on them. That one is like a man building a house, who dug deeply and laid the foundation on rock; when a flood arose, the river burst against that house but could not shake it, because it had been well built. But the one who hears and does not act is like a man who built a house on the ground without a foundation. When the river burst against it, immediately it fell, and great was the ruin of that house.
>
> (Luke 6:47-49)

Tuning In: Ways to discover issues of loss and crisis among youth

Below are exercises you as an adult worker can use to become more attuned to the struggle with loss and crisis that youth experience.

- *Brainstorm topics.* Have the youth brainstorm a list of topics they want to explore that would help them be better prepared to support their friends who are going through hard times. Get the ball rolling with ideas such as divorce, death of a loved one, handling stress, conflict resolution, forgiveness, and so forth. Some of the suggestions will be issues that the youth themselves are facing. See the "List of Topics" (pages 157-158) for additional ideas.

- *Do some reading.* Introduce the youth to authors such as Elisabeth Kubler-Ross, whose books discuss stages of grief and loss. (See "For Further Reading" on page155 for more information.) Have the youth write in their journals about a time when they went through stages of grief or loss in their own lives. Encourage the youth who are willing to discuss with trusted adults or a group of peers what they have written in their journals.

- *Do roleplaying.* Have the youth create roleplays about positive ways people can cope with major losses and crises in their lives. Have them define *loss* and *crisis.*

- *Get to know other youth who struggle.* Scan school newsletters, community newspapers, church bulletins, and so forth for indications of hard times in the lives of youth you know and youth you don't know, and/or their families.

- *Name people who need support.* Several times a year, ask the youth to identify one other young person they know who is struggling with loss or with handling a crisis. Give the youth time to pray for that person and to consider one way they might be supportive of that person.

- *Utilize videos and songs that highlight people who are facing hardship.* Discuss the messages that those videos or songs are conveying. Ask the youth to discuss what they see as real in these images. Ask them where they will get their support when times get rough.

Twists of Faith: Activities that make a faith connection

Use the following activities to help youth connect their faith in God with experiences of loss or crisis in their own lives and in the lives of their friends and families.

Encourage Testimonies

Invite adults and other youth of faith who have faced losses and crises of various kinds to come and talk with your youth group. Ask these people to tell how they got through these experiences and how God's presence sustained them through the struggles. Make sure you know the content of the testimonies before the youth do, so you can be sure that what is being said will be helpful.

Sing Songs of Faith and Hope

Lead the youth in singing songs that have faith and hope as their themes. Afterwards, divide the group into pairs. Have each pair meditate on the words of each song in silence, then discuss their reflections with their partner. Pairs may consider questions such as: "What do you think the songwriter was trying to say? Which parts of the song do you agree with? Which parts would you say in a different way?"

Compare Scripture

Have the youth compare Psalm 22 and Psalm 23. Ask: "What are the similarities and differences between the way these two psalms (which are back to back in the Bible) approach difficult times and express faith in God?"

Create a "Signs of Hope" Box

In the top of a box, cut a hole one inch wide and twelve inches long. Decorate the box. For four weeks, have the youth gather articles, pictures, poems, songs, and so forth that convey a sense of hope; also ask the youth to write down every act or situation they observe that they consider a sign of hope for them personally or for the world. Each week ask the youth to drop what they have gathered or written into the box. Use these thoughts, reflections, and insights as resources for worship experiences, conversation starters, prayers, newsletters, bulletin covers, and more.

Create a Youth Altar

Have the youth create an altar where they can bring the joys and concerns in their lives to God. Make sure it is in a place where the person can find solitude to pray and to reflect. Have play dough and art supplies of all kinds available at the altar so the youth who choose to can make visible symbols to represent what is on their hearts. Create a tradition of having the youth leave on the altar the symbols they have created for as long as these symbols are pertinent to their lives and to create as many as they wish. Gather around the altar as a youth group each week for silent prayer. Following silent prayer, offer the opportunity for youth to ask for group prayer related to a joy, concern, or celebration of God's presence in their lives. Those who are willing may explain to the group the meaning of the symbol or symbols he or she has created. You may also offer the opportunity for individuals who prefer to come to you or other trusted adults to explain a symbol and its meaning.

Read and Discuss Mark 14:32-43

With the whole group, discuss the passage using questions like these: "What does it mean for us that Jesus had hard times and sometimes felt forsaken? Did Jesus still have faith after experiencing such feelings? How do you know?"

SEARCH FOR MEANING & PURPOSE

CHAPTER 11

First Glance

Before reading this chapter, reflect on these thoughts:

Not even suffering can steal the heart of those who know that they have something meaningful to contribute.

I came that they may have life, and have it abundantly.
(John 10:10b)

Heart to Heart

This chapter provides adult workers with insights and tools for engaging youth in discovering a guiding purpose for their lives. Keep in mind, this endeavor takes a significant amount of time. Youth will need breaks from the normal routine of their lives, along with places devoid of distractions, in order to get to know themselves. You will be asking them to pause and to listen for the "inner voice"—the nudging of the Spirit. New insights they glean from the process of seeking meaning create a foundation for establishing vision and direction for their own lives.

How about your own life as leader? Before you read the rest of the chapter, find a time and place where you can ponder the following questions: What inspires you to keep getting out of bed morning after morning? How would you describe the deepest purpose of your life? What are your central values? List those people or those aspects of your life that bring you joy. What contributions do you make that have meaning for you and for others? Describe your aspirations—your hopes for the future.

For some of us, such introspection may be an uncomfortable exercise. Instead of confirming a depth of meaning, it may expose its absence during this time in your life. Don't be overly discouraged; we have experienced this too. Your recognition of the absence of meaning and purpose can be the impetus for a change in your life. Take the crucial first steps to break free of the inertia that holds you in the status quo. The tension between what is and what you feel called toward can be a good thing. This is also true for the youth.

Whether you have a clear sense of purpose, or whether you are unsure, seek God. God is faithful. God knows you better than you know yourself. God understands your uniqueness. Join in this prayer written by a fellow seeker:

> O LORD, you have searched me and known me.
> You know when I sit down and when I rise up;
>   you discern my thoughts from far away.
> You search out my path and my lying down,
>   and are acquainted with all my ways.
> Even before a word is on my tongue,
>   O LORD, you know it completely, . . .
> If I say, "Surely the darkness shall cover me,
>   and the light around me become night,"
> even the darkness is not dark to you;
>   the night is as bright as the day,
>   for darkness is as light to you.
> For it was you who formed my inward parts;
>   you knit me together in my mother's womb.
> I praise you, for I am fearfully and wonderfully made.
>   Wonderful are your works . . .
> Search me, O God, and know my heart;
>   test me and know my thoughts.
> See if there is any wicked way in me,
>   and lead me in the way everlasting.
>   (Psalm 139:1-4, 11-14, 23-24)

Spend time talking with God about the direction of your life and pray for specific young people you care about who do not seem to have a sense of purpose.

 Real Life: Stories drawn from the lives of youth

 Which Way Now?

Things have been strange lately. People have been coming up to me—a teacher, my camp dean, a friend—and have complimented me about how well I speak in front of groups. It surprised me and made me happy. I like to talk about what's important in life and to get people to think. I will be heading for college soon. One of these people asked me if I ever considered teaching or being a minister. She really urged me to consider that possibility.

That would be a big shift. I chose my college, starting this fall, because of its awesome biology department. Throughout my life, nature and wild creatures brought me tremendous joy. I always felt close to God in the midst of the natural world. Science opened up a world that fascinated me. I figured that my plan to become a wildlife biologist and work for the Fish and Game Department fit perfectly with who I am.

Now I'm not so sure. I feel a little frustrated and excited at the same time. I'm not as positive as before about which way to go. I wish I could know for certain what is the right path for me. Somehow I feel God calling me, but where? and to do what? Is the college I have chosen to attend this fall the right one? Everything is set up there. What if I make a mistake and choose wrong?

**It
Scares
Me**

Why don't I seem to be excited about anything anymore? My friends all have stuff they are pumped about. I see people getting involved. They talk about and fight for causes that mean a lot to them. The issues they care about pretty much bore me. It's not that I'm a jerk. I really want to care about something but can't seem to conjure up whatever it is that these other people have.

My teachers tell me to watch the news so I'll know what is going on in the world. I'm taught that we have a responsibility to read the paper and keep up with things, if we care about society. I try watching and reading, but I have a hard time keeping it up.

All this scares me. I feel like there might be something wrong with me. I'm a nice enough person. Why don't I care more? To tell you the truth, it's sort of lonely, even though I have friends. I could be involved, but I haven't found anything that inspires me. Am I screwed up, or is this normal sometimes?

**A
Funeral
in My
Future?**

Ever since I was a little kid, I loved funerals. I remember using my brothers' and sisters' action figures and dolls to create elaborate funeral ceremonies. Using my imagination, the dolls spoke about fallen comrades and why they would be missed. It didn't feel weird to me. The local funeral home was just down the street from my house, so I hung out there sometimes. The people who owned it befriended me. They liked me.

I even went to funerals of people I didn't even know. People seemed genuinely grateful to the funeral home staff, and even hugged them. Something was happening there that struck me as very important. When I was older, I once attended the funeral of a relative in another town. The mortician was cranky and kind of mean. *Wow! He's not helping*, I thought. *He's making it harder for the family and friends.* At that moment, I realized that being a good funeral director could really make a difference to people at a critical time in their lives. I could bring some comfort and hope where it's needed.

I'm absolutely sure I am supposed to be a funeral home director.
That's my calling.

Questions: How would you respond to these youth if they came to talk with you? What faith connections might apply in these situations?

Delving Deeper

Youth long to know that their lives matter. Many stand ready to search deeply in order to discover reasons for being that they recognize as valuable. That is an essential point to comprehend. A youth does not thrive simply because other people think that his or her presence matters. Young people thrive when they perceive a purpose for their lives that they themselves consider important.

Never underestimate the capacity of young people to reflect on the purpose of their own lives. Most senior high and many junior high students need spiritual mentors who supply processes for exploring how their uniqueness and passions can contribute to enriching the world. The search for meaning and purpose should not be relegated solely to adulthood; it begins in earnest during adolescence—for some, even in childhood. Adult leaders give youth a major leg up in life when they honor this youthful search for meaning and purpose.

Long-term doubt about whether or not one's life has a point drags a person down toward gloom and despair. Frequently people try to fill the void with inadequate substitutes, but these pale in comparison to the fullness of knowing that "my life makes a difference." Groping for a more satisfying existence, some individuals attempt to control others. Others seek solace in leisure or immediate gratification, or try to avoid introspection by maintaining a busy schedule. Still others try to satisfy their inner emptiness by gathering more and more possessions. Some of these conscious or unconscious strategies are insidiously deceptive because they temporarily cover up the underlying hollowness.

The key word here is *temporarily,* because emptiness, whether dressed up or ignored, does not go away. But life *does* drain away. We see the dissipation of life in many forms, ranging from replacing real existence with staring at a television screen or playing video games for hours every day to, at the extreme, suicide. These signs of lethargy or distress are common among teenagers.

What are the potential sources that regularly quench people's thirst for meaning? Name these wellsprings for yourself, so you can help youth to identify them. Take the young people to these oases of meaning, so that they can gain the resources to energize them and call forth the best in them.

Let's discuss some of the sources of meaning and purpose.

Sources of Meaning

Inspirations. The word *inspiration* derives from the word *spirit*. Scripture connects the Spirit (God) closely with the "breath of life," or with being alive. Appreciating oneself as a precious child of a gracious God grants a sense of worth that others cannot steal. Connecting with the Source of life that never ends secures a future of lasting hope. The endeavor to grow more in tune with the love of God offers a reason for existence that satisfies, up to the very moment of our death—and beyond. God will inspire young people and quench their thirst for meaning. Encourage youth to seek God, the Source of life's meaning.

Inspiration also comes from values. Values lead to ways of being that naturally produce life within relationships and creation.

Here are a few examples of values: freedom for all, justice, trustworthiness, loving even one's enemies, stewardship of the earth, slowness to anger, ingenuity, truthfulness, compassion, forgiveness, creating beauty, and peacefulness. These values find expression in some of the most stirring and energizing passages of Scripture, poetry, music, writings, and art forms known to humanity; and thousands of people are motivated by these.

Relationships. Relationships typically furnish energy and purpose. Being a truly good parent, soulmate, or friend represents remarkable reasons for being. Purpose is derived from participating in faith communities, teams, and other groups where members truly know, honor, and unite with one another in mutually beneficial support and outreach.

Contributions. Individuals find immense joy when they detect a need that they can ease or satisfy. We shouldn't fall into the trap of always portraying such deeds as the grand causes that receive great notoriety. Impress upon the youth that a gracious smile or the gift of laughter, for instance, represent an awesome gift that can bring healing to a family or a stranger. We bless our youth by expanding their appreciation of the sacred value of simple gestures. Youth may act, also, by funneling portions of their money and assets to benefit those in need.

Passions. Meaning flows from ongoing enthusiasm drawn from a specific activity or concept. An idea that captures

The Samaritan woman said to him, "How is it that you, a Jew, ask a drink of me, a woman of Samaria?" (Jews do not share things in common with Samaritans.) Jesus answered her, "If you knew the gift of God, and who it is that is saying to you, 'Give me a drink,' you would have asked him, and he would have given you living water . . . [T]hose who drink of the water that I will give them will never be thirsty. The water that I will give will become in them a spring of water gushing up to eternal life." The woman said to him, "Sir, give me this water."

(John 4:9-10, 14-15a)

the imagination can impel people to great heights. One woman humbly led dozens of inner-city youth to new frontiers, because it came to her that involving them in tending gardens of their own throughout their neighborhoods might put them in touch with their own creativity and beauty. The simple notion of "conflict resolution" triggered some consequential careers. Keep your eye out for youth who seem moved by such themes. A mission related to these concepts may somehow germinate for their lives, if the youth can figure out a way to apply these to real life.

Others spend hours pursuing particular activities that challenge them and bring them joy. Teaching children, riding horses, doing gymnastics, playing softball, drawing, dancing, fly fishing, talking on the phone, gardening, and cooking for friends are drops in an ocean of possibilities. When youth use their ardor to do good and to grow as people themselves, they tap into meaning.

Recognitions. Sometimes God uses a talent or skill we have as a clue to new sources of meaning. Encourage the youth to boldly assess the diversity of their talents and the skills at which they excel. Some of these talents and skills seem so natural to the teenagers that, at first, they may not even grasp these as gifts. Other skills require great effort to hone, yet the young person ends up doing these well. Pay especially close attention to aptitudes that folks who know the youth well also recognize; such recognition affirms the young person's own judgment about his or her gifts.

Aspirations and creations. A vision or goal is a potent force that impels people into the future. A vision or goal paints a picture of a future to aspire to. Meaning comes in trying to create something that does not now exist or in preparing for experiences yet unfulfilled. These aspirations and creations do not need to be totally unique to be meaningful. Terminally ill patients, at times, live far beyond expectations just so they can hold a newborn child or grandchild. Average athletes may strive for years to know what it's like to play or to score in a single high school game. Exerting oneself to reach a worthy goal generates a sense of joy and purpose. Some people scrimp and save in order to take a trip to another country or even to attend a much-anticipated week of camp. Others experiment with gadgets that improve an already existing machine, and this gives them great satisfaction.

Life flies by. So let's tutor youth to reflect on and to clarify their dreams and visions, either by writing these down in a journal or by articulating them in another way. Once the youth have identified the visions, goals, and aspirations for their lives and have been able to see these clearly, they can take concrete steps toward making them happen.

> Some give freely,
> yet grow all the richer;
> others withhold what is due, and only suffer want.
> A generous person will be enriched,
> and one who gives water will get water.
> (Proverbs 11:24-25)

Vocations. An extended focus to which one feels truly called fuels a sense of purpose. People may have a number of vocations in a lifetime. Dedicating a great deal of time and energy to endeavors that are simultaneously intriguing and beneficial to the community can create significant meaning in the life of a youth. Young people deserve numerous opportunities to discern a vocation. They need support from others in preparing for a chosen field of service. But the choice of vocation should never be left solely or even predominantly to the discretion of others—it should be the youth's own decision.

Ideally, vocations provide the income necessary to earn a living; however, this may not always be the case. Raising one's own children well is a tremendous vocation, but is not always matched by the compensation it deserves! Making a living is necessary, but spiritual teachers of many faiths have long warned that accumulating money in and of itself is not a worthy endeavor. Sadly, many people spend the bulk of their waking hours doing tasks far removed from the center of their being—solely for financial income. At the end of their lives, these unfortunate people look back with regret, feeling that they have never truly lived. We bless youth when we bolster creativity and advocate balance in figuring out how to pursue meaning while at the same time meeting life's basic needs and wants.

A popular falsehood permeates mainline culture in the United States of America. Advertisements bombard our psyches, promising us happiness if only we would buy a particular product, store up large amounts of wealth for ourselves and our children, and buy objects that give pleasure. The intent of almost all advertising is to make us feel inadequate or deprived. They know that only by creating this sense of want or lack will people buy their products. Both adults and young people repeatedly swallow and get hooked on this lie. Adult workers can offer valuable biblical wisdom and guidance, for example:

> For where your treasure is, there your heart will be also.   (Matthew 6:21)

> And [Jesus] said to them, "Take care! Be on your guard against all kinds of greed; for one's life does not consist in the abundance of possessions." Then he told them a parable: "The land of a rich man produced abundantly. And he thought to himself, 'What should I do, for I have no place to store my crops?' Then he said, 'I will do this: I will pull down my barns and build larger ones, and there I will store all my grain and my goods. And I will say to my soul, "Soul, you have ample goods laid up for many years; relax, eat, drink, be merry." ' But God said to him, 'You fool! This very night your life is being demanded of you. And the things you have prepared, whose will they be?' So it is with those who store up treasures for themselves but are not rich toward God."   (Luke 12:15-21)

Before leaving this discussion of wellsprings of meaning, we would like to direct your attention to the profound writings of Victor Frankl. A Jew, Frankl was a highly trained psychologist who ended up as a prisoner in Nazi concentration camps during the Holocaust. Under the bleakest conditions of deprivation, he noticed that the prisoners who survived were not the ones with the most physical strength, but rather those who maintained a sense of purpose and meaning for their lives. In his books, Frankl discusses some of the sources of meaning he beheld among the prisoners. One of his landmark observations was that even severe suffering itself could become a source of meaning. We urge you to read Frankl's classic book, *Man's Search for Meaning*, in which he artfully tells about his experiences. (See "For Further Reading" for more information about Frankl's book.)

Tuning In:
Ways to help youth discover sources of meaning and purpose

- *Make palettes of meaning.* A painter uses a palette that holds a small supply of many different colors of paint. The painter chooses the colors and what he or she will create with these various colors. In the same way, youth can become co-creators with God. Like the "Divine Painter," we too express our lives in various ways. The following exercise helps youth learn to paint a life of meaning.

  Provide each youth with an 8 1/2-by-11 sheet of paper and ask the youth to write "Painting From the Heart" at the top of the sheet. Next, have the youth draw the painter's palette as large as possible directly below the title. (Display a copy of the diagram of the palette found on this page for the youth to consult. Alternatively, you can prepare the diagram yourself and make photocopies for each member of the group.) Provide the youth with crayons, markers, pens, and other art supplies for completing the exercise. Briefly explain to the group what is meant by "sources of meaning" (see pages 126–130). Also explain the meaning of the three paintbrushes on the palette: The first brush stands for seeking God: How am I going to seek God? The second brush stands for becoming more loving: What am I going to do to allow myself to be an artist who will paint from the heart? The third paintbrush symbolizes helping God: How can I participate with what God is doing in my life? Ask the group to remember the meaning of the three brushes as they complete the exercise.

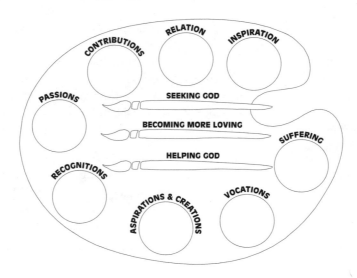

Next, invite everyone to write words or phrases, or to draw symbols, in each paint circle on the palette in response to the ideas or questions below for each circle:

Inspiration circle: How do you seek God's guidance in creating or discovering a meaningful life for yourself? How does being a follower of God make life more worthwhile? What poems, sayings, ideas, or Scripture references inspire you? What moves you to get out of bed each day?

Relation circle: What relationships do you now have that enrich your life? What could you do to create a better family life? Who are the important people in your life? What kinds of relationships do you want in the future?

Contributions circle: What major needs in the world would you like to help solve or to ease? What small acts of kindness would make life better for you, the people around you, or the earth?

Passions circle: What do you have enthusiasm for? How can you use what interests you—your passions—to make a difference? How do you spend your free time when you get to choose? What do you enjoy?

Recognitions circle: What do you feel you're good or skilled at? What do others say you're good or skilled at? How can these activities and gifts bring you and others joy?

Aspirations and Creations circle: What are your hopes for the future? Meaning comes in preparing for a new experience or creating something new that is worthwhile. What are you working toward? What are some things you would like to experience before you die? What do you like to create?

Vocations circle: Earning money does not create meaning at all. In fact, the pursuit of money can easily distract us from what is truly meaningful. What kinds of things do you see yourself doing for many years that would give your life meaning? How likely is it that you could earn a living doing what God calls you to do? If this is unlikely, how will you continue to do what nurtures your soul and gives you meaning when your job does not provide that nurture and meaning?

Suffering circle: Experiences you go through, regardless of whether they are menial or difficult, help to develop who you are as a person. Illness, disasters, or ongoing hardship can deeply affect who you become. How can even these experiences become a source of meaning and give you purpose in your life?

- *Start meaning diaries.* Cut sheets of white paper into five-by-eleven-inch strips. Put three sheets together, fold them in half, and staple them at the fold. Make enough of the diaries so each member of the youth group will have one. Give the youth art supplies to decorate the front and back covers of their diaries. The covers should consist of scenes or symbols representing a meaningful experience or experiences drawn from the youth's own life story. They should leave the inside front and back covers blank. The remaining eight pages are for recording thoughts and reflections.

  Ask the youth to make an entry in their diaries every day for eight days, confining each entry to a single page. (If you are doing this exercise during a weekend retreat, give the youth a time frame that enables them to complete the entries over the course of the weekend.) Every entry should consist of a brief description of a time or incident in the life of the youth that he or she found particularly meaningful. At least one third of each entry should outline why the event or incident was meaningful.

At the end of the eight-day period, have the youth talk with one another about what they have learned about themselves from this exercise. Specifically, ask the youth to discuss ways in which meaningful events or times in their past have provided clues for gaining meaning in the future. Have all the youth who feel comfortable doing so turn their diaries in to you. Tell the youth you would like to collect the diaries so that you can learn about what they consider important for their lives; in this way, you can be more understanding and supportive.

Twists of Faith: Activities that make a faith connection

Use the following activity to help youth connect their faith in God with their quest for meaning and purpose.

Dare to Dream

Have the young people read the first chapter of Genesis. Discuss the chapter in the following way: Reread out loud every verse that begins, "And [or Then] God said . . ." Ask the youth: "Did these things—light, animals, plants, and so forth—already exist at the time that God was talking about them?" (*The answer is no.*) God saw these realities *before* they existed in the same way that we can imagine things that do not yet exist and can talk about them. Genesis 1:27 indicates that human beings are made in God's image; that means human beings have the power to co-create with God and have the responsibility to do so lovingly.

Ask: "What role does imagination play in creating? Is imagination by itself enough to make something happen? Martin Luther King, Jr. once said that he had a dream. How did his dream for the future differ from the reality he found himself in? What concrete steps did people have to take to help make King's dream come true?"

Have the young people individually and quietly ponder the meaning of the two questions below for their own lives. Then have them write their responses to the questions on a sheet of paper.

1. What dreams do you have for yourself? for the world? What do you want your life to say? Complete this sentence: "And _____ (*youth's name*) said . . ."
2. Prayerfully write down at least five concrete steps you are willing to take to help make happen the dream you identified above. Complete this sentence: "Dear God, I promise to . . ." (*List the five steps.*) in order to fulfill this dream. (*Describe the dream concisely.*) Please give me the wisdom and tenacity to be a loving co-creator with You so that I may make my own life and the world better."

Pair each teenager with another youth or with an adult. Have the youth share their statement (under number 2 above) with one another and to make a copy of the statement for their partner. The partner's role is that of encouragement and of reminding and supporting the other person in the commitment to his or her dream. Plan times for the partners to get together over the next year to report progress and challenges.

FAMILY EXPERIENCES

irst Glance

Before reading this chapter, reflect on this thought:

Children, obey your parents in the Lord, for this is right.

"Honor your father and mother"—this is the first commandment with a promise: "so that it may be well with you and you may live long on the earth." And, fathers, do not provoke your children to anger, but bring them up in the discipline and instruction of the Lord.   (Ephesians 6:1-4)

Heart to Heart

Let's be real: Family remains the number one influence in the lives of most youth. Peers, school, and the church have an impact on teenagers, but generally speaking, not to the same degree as their home life. If adult leaders truly desire to enrich the lives of young people, they will strengthen the families of the youth.

Reread the passage above from Ephesians 6:1-4; then take time to ponder these questions.

- Has it been easy to honor your own father and/or mother? Why or why not?
- When did you experience the most difficult periods in the relationship with your parent(s)?
- As an older teen or adult, were you able to establish your own identity while maintaining a loving relationship with your parents or guardians? If so, how did you accomplish this? If not, based on your present perspective, what would have contributed to a better outcome?
  - Where was God in all this?
  - How did or how could the church have made a difference for you and your family?
  - How might you enhance the mutual honor that nurtures family ties for the youth with whom you work?

Conclude your reflections with this prayer: "God, remind me to embrace parent(s), siblings, and extended family members as part of my concern for youth. Please direct my ways and my words through your wisdom and insight, in order to draw them closer to you and your love. Amen." And remember: All youth need a nurturing home base.

Real Life: Stories drawn from the lives of youth

The Prayer-a-Thon

Prayer boxes collected from various locations now held the prayer requests of churchgoers, families, and friends. Heartwarming celebrations and heart-wrenching concerns spilled onto the table. Delivering these communiqués to God would be the focus of the youth group for the next twelve hours. The youth buzzed with genuine excitement.

The majority of parents dropped their sons and daughters off, then quickly departed. One parent, however, lingered near the doorway; this drew my attention. "I wrote out my prayer request a few days ago and put it in the box here at the church," he said. "Great! Thanks for participating and making the effort to bring your kids tonight. We are eager to get started," I replied.

He stood quietly for a moment. With glistening eyes, he looked at me and said, "You've *already* started. You see, my sister and I have been estranged for over twenty years. She refused to speak to me or return my phone calls, though I kept trying to make contact. So I wrote out my request asking for prayers that God would somehow reunite us and begin to heal our relationship." He swallowed hard, then continued, "She called me this morning. We actually talked with each other. And I want all of you to know that because of the youth's invitation to write prayer requests, my prayers have been heard and answered. I can't begin to adequately express our gratitude. Will you please share this with the youth and thank them?"

She Would Not Speak

Maria never spoke. Day after day, the teachers tried to break her silence through classroom conversation and activities, but to no avail. School officials alerted her mother to the situation. The mother posed some suggestions that might help Maria. These alternatives, however, fell outside the bounds of the usual way of doing things, so the teachers resisted. Some considered the mother herself to be part of the problem rather than part of the solution. Few welcomed or respected this woman. In the meantime, the child continued her voiceless vigil.

One of the school counselors decided to pursue a new solution to this dilemma. She called the staff and teachers who were directly involved with Maria to a consultation. She asked these educators point blank, "Do you really want what's best for this child?" They cautiously nodded in affirmation. "We are in a bind here. The mother blames the school, and the school blames the family. I know that many of you prefer to avoid Maria's mom because of her criticism. You may even resent her presence. Our strategies apart from the parent have failed to draw this child out, however. I want us to reverse course and forge an alliance with Maria's mother."

Initially, this approach received little support. Eventually, though, Maria's mother was invited to join them at the school to discuss working together as partners for Maria's sake. This ultimately meant having the mother present from time to time at class itself.

The teachers and staff got to know the mother better. They treated her more kindly and respectfully. When this happened, Maria almost miraculously started talking. She participated fully, and her grades jumped. She quickly made friends with other students. She blossomed. Cooperation and honor transformed this child in a way that can only be described as remarkable.

My Mother Taught Me

My mother never said much about the Bible. Instead, she lived it; she walked it; she breathed it. Her kind, gentle demeanor revealed a faith that was strong and steady.

At a very young age, I received a Bible at Sunday school with my name on it. While the other kids carried their Bibles around and seemed a little confused about what to do with them, I picked up my Bible and began reading. I wasn't sure what part to read, but that didn't matter. I did what I had observed my mother do every day of her life. I imitated her practice even before I could fully understand the words.

As I got older, Mom wrote down meaningful passages and quietly left them on the kitchen counter or handed them directly to me without fanfare. When I moved away from home, she included them in letters she mailed to me. She found ways to share what mattered most to her. Her lifelong theme centered on God's love for us all. It never struck me as artificial.

The foundation that my mother helped build in my faith almost went unnoticed because it was so routine. But that routine modeled a pattern of learning, growing, searching, hoping, and reaching out in partnership with God; that became our family life. Even though my mom is no longer living, she continues to shape me. I look back on my youth with immense gratitude.

Question: What do these stories reveal about the importance of partnering with families to build up youth, both personally and spiritually?

Thought: The better we know and honor our youth and their family members, the more influence we are granted to encourage faith connections in their lives.

Delving Deeper

In her best-selling book, *The Shelter of Each Other: Rebuilding Our Families*, Mary Pipher describes powerful forces in society today that weaken families. She encourages families to unite more consciously to resist the influences that threaten to tear them apart. As a well-known youth and family therapist, Pipher sees firsthand the devastation of broken families and the beauty of bonds of love. She speaks of the changing landscape within our culture and offers strategies to build strong homes. Her experience leads her to conclude unequivocally that youth need strong families. Family life makes a huge difference during the twists and turns of a person's life.[1]

Two insights from Pipher's book have particular import for spiritual leaders of youth. First, a bent toward extreme individualism and the longing for easy answers create an atmosphere in which families get blamed as the sole cause of the problems and messes the youth get into. Youth sometimes buy into this victim mentality, thinking that the cause for their behavior has to do with the way they were brought up, and therefore, that their upbringing has created their present misery. Thus, since they perceive their families as having negatively influenced their lives, the logical solution for many young people is to rebel or to separate from the main influences of parents or siblings.

Unfortunately many professional counselors, and even friends, regularly elevate individual happiness above all other concerns, including the need for the youth to take responsibility for his or her own actions—actions that may have contributed to the personal and family malaise. The irony is that this kind of counseling is blind to the truth that improving family life itself contributes to personal happiness. So, as an initial and primary strategy, why not emphasize strengthening family life over advocating that the youth separate from parent(s) and siblings? After all, no family is perfect, and young people still need families.

Second, families today are invaded by distractions and activities that are inclined to disrupt relationships. Observe a room full of people watching television. Notice that they pay little or no attention to each other at all. They think they are together, but in reality each person slips into his or her own little world. Or take the frantic striving of many parents to gain material security and to better the lives of their children. Such pursuits may harm the children, because they get possessions rather than relationships, which are more valuable.

---

1 See *The Shelter of Each Other: Rebuilding Our Families,* by Mary Pipher (Ballantine Books, 1996).

At one time, family members worked side by side to accomplish the daily tasks of life, but that is not nearly so true today. Many teenagers have schedules that are even busier than their parents'! A myriad of activities, previously unimagined, draws them away from interaction with family.

There are several ways for adult workers with youth to channel the grace of God into the family "mix." Below are a few of the more important ways.

1. *Teach relational skills.* It's amazing how a little shared knowledge improves interactions, sometimes dramatically. We should not assume that youth or adults know the techniques that enhance bonding and interactions. Some of these skills are learned. Attentive listening, group planning, conflict-resolution techniques, parent-youth dialogues, and so forth frequently open new streams of communication and mutual appreciation.

2. *Facilitate reconciliation.* Adult leaders must avoid being lulled into accepting the stance that teenagers will inevitably not get along with their parents, guardians or siblings, because the natural process of growing up requires this. First of all, few youth ever really want to be alienated from their family. Youth desire good relationships with those close to them. Second, our faith advises us to seek reconciliation and to restore right relationships, whenever possible, for this enriches existence. The story of Jacob and Esau serves as a poignant illustration. (See Genesis, chapters 25-28, 32-33.)

   God can work in even the most unlikely circumstances. Jacob and Esau struggled through their growing-up years. As adults, this rivalry reached extreme proportions. On one occasion, Jacob refused to give a famished Esau some food unless Esau agreed to sell his birthright to Jacob. Esau frivolously consented. Their parents contributed to the intrigue of deception and manipulation, which for years left the two brothers completely antagonistic toward each other. Not even Jacob could imagine the forgiveness his brother Esau would later bestow upon him in one of the most dramatic, touching accounts of reconciliation recorded in the Bible. Jacob sums up his heartfelt reaction: "[F]or truly to see your face is like seeing the face of God—since you have received me with such favor" (Genesis 33:10b). Think about the years of agony that could have been avoided had a caring adult stepped into the lives of these men when they were young and had offered support and a new perspective to the family.

3. *Honor the variety of families.* Teenagers hesitate to introduce adult leaders to their families, especially when they feel that the type of family they have does not meet the adult worker's approval. These intended or unintended messages creep in subtly, so adult leaders must deliberately show respect. For example, when speaking about the variety of family arrangements, will everyone in your youth groups find his or her family included?

   Certain images of the family in the Bible break with the typical American image of the family: father, mother, and 1.5 children. For example, Jesus himself never married; and some people today view God as a single parent. Consider these additional examples from Scripture.

At this time Moses was born, and he was beautiful before God. For three months he was brought up in his father's house; and when he was abandoned, Pharaoh's daughter adopted him and brought him up as her own son.   (Acts 7:20-21)

Blessed be the God and Father of our Lord Jesus Christ, who has blessed us in Christ with every spiritual blessing in the heavenly places, just as he chose us in Christ before the foundation of the world to be holy and blameless before him in love. He destined us for adoption as his children through Jesus Christ, according to the good pleasure of his will, to the praise of his glorious grace that he freely bestowed on us in the Beloved.   (Ephesians 1:3-6)

Ruth chose her mother-in-law, Naomi, as her family.
"Do not press me to leave you
    or to turn back from following you!
Where you go, I will go;
    Where you lodge, I will lodge;
your people shall be my people,
    and your God my God.
Where you die, I will die—
    there will I be buried."

(Ruth 1:16-17a)

The point is: *God moves in all families.*

4. *Partner with families.* Too often ministry with youth happens apart from their families. This is not to say that adults and other siblings in the family need to be involved in every youth activity. Probably neither the teenager nor the family members would want or expect that. However, efforts should be made, whenever feasible, to incorporate the youth's family members in youth activities. Consider these suggestions:

   • Invite the family member or friend who has arrived to drive the youth home to join the youth circle for the closing prayer. This gesture makes an important statement about who is included in the group and who sits on the sidelines.

   • Learn the names of family members and greet them personally when you see them.

   • Provide resources and suggestions about how families can grow closer to God in their home setting. Such resources tell youth that faith matters in everyday life, not just on Sundays.

   • Be clear that you are working as a partner with families to support their sons and daughters in personal and spiritual growth. (See "For Further Reading" on page 155 for suggested resources; note especially the book *Capture the Moment: Building Faith Traditions for Families,* by Rick and Sue Isbell.)

5. *Be there in times of need:* It may surprise you how often the family members of one of the youth will trust adult youth leaders in difficult times, especially when the leader has shown that he or she cares for the entire family. A loving presence can mean so much to the family. Sending a card to an adult family member whose parent has died, while also consoling the youth who has lost a grandparent, sends the clear message that your concern as youth leader extends to the whole family.

6. *Engage community intervention, when necessary:* In severe cases, such as overwhelming loss, suspicion of abuse, threats of suicide, and so forth, a family needs professional help beyond what the adult worker can provide. (See Chapter 5, "It's Beyond Me!" for a discussion on when to seek the help of other professionals.)

We need to be careful not to make assumptions about the home life of youth we work with. Consequently, it is especially important that we get to know families well in order to develop an effective and appropriate ministry with them. Youth ministry as family ministry definitely takes more time, but it pays dividends. Keep in mind that our purpose stays constant: to assist people in developing a deeper relationship with God and in learning to live as Christian disciples.

 Tuning In: Ways to learn more about youth and their families

The activities below may help you as an adult worker to learn more about your youth and their families, as well as how to be in ministry with them.

- *Start a support group.* Seek out a trained counselor or other qualified person to start a support group for recently divorced people and their children. Some congregations have started such groups and have transformed many lives for the better. You will want to open it up to the community as well as to church members. This tells hurting families in the community that your congregation is a place of acceptance for them and their children.

- *Visit youth in their homes.* Brainstorm with the youth about activities for the youth that could be hosted in the homes of youth members. The activity could be simple, such as enjoying a meal together; or it could take the form of an elaborate program. Being in the home of a youth member could have multiple benefits. First, it involves the youth's family. Second, the change of location stimulates interest among the youth. Third, it gives the adult leader a non-threatening opportunity to see where a teenager lives, to experience a bit of the dynamics of the home, and maybe to gain hints about what is important to the youth and other family members. Remember: Get the adult family member's or members' approval and invitation in advance of scheduling a youth activity in a home.

- *Organize a family mega-group night.* Those who work with youth groups can guide the youth in planning and leading a "family activity and celebration" evening for all the families of the youth. Someone can be assigned to take photographs of the families, while others lead the evening's program of family activities. Put the photographs up on a hallway bulletin board for the congregation to see, thus introducing the youth and their families to congregation members.

- *Offer a class for parents of teenagers.* Some parents and guardians will welcome a chance to learn parenting skills, family faith-formation models, how to develop strong relationships, and so forth. Conversing with other parents also can be valuable. Work with your church or camp staff to offer a class or retreat for parents (or perhaps for youth and their parents/guardians together). Preparing, teaching, or simply participating in such an event will offer you new insights about everyone involved and thus increase your effectiveness as an adult worker with youth.

- *Conduct a survey of parents.* Ask parents to participate in a survey that asks questions about them as individuals, as well as about their family patterns. Include a section in which participants are asked to complete statements like the following.

Two things I love about my family are
1. _____
2. _____
The one thing about my family that I wish could be different is _____

_____

One thing I especially like about my child(ren) is _____

_____

One way in which the church supports my child(ren) and our family is

_____

One thing I would like the church to do, which it is not now doing, that would support our family is _____

_____

The favorite activity our family likes to share in is _____

_____

 Twists of Faith: Activities that make a faith connection

Use the following activities to help youth connect their faith in God with the relationships they maintain with their families.

What Would It Be Like?

(This activity is best suited for older youth.)

Divide the youth group into small groups of two or three. Provide them with pencils and a list of questions. Ask each person to complete the questionnaire below, then share the answers with members of his or her small group. Use the following questions:

- If you were the parent of a teenager:

1. What would you do to be the "ideal" parent?

2. What house rules or requirements would you keep, and which would you change?

3. How could you encourage your teenage son or daughter to talk with you about important issues?

4. What advice could you give your son or daughter about getting along better with their siblings and/or friends?

5. If you were to list some things that you feel your parents did right in raising you, what would these be?

6. What are some ways in which your family could share thoughts and feelings about God with one another on a consistent basis? What might you do to recognize and welcome God in your family practices?

Reassemble the whole group and have someone from each small group share highlights. Encourage the youth to have empathy for the difficult job of being a parent or guardian. Have each youth create a thank-you card for his or her parent(s) or guardian(s), with some specific reasons why he or she is thankful for this adult.

Watch the Clock

Make a chart for the youth to track the time they spend doing various activities with their families. Be sure the chart includes a specific beginning and ending time for tracking the activities. (One week is reasonable.) Include items on the chart such as:

- Time spent daily with screens (television, computer, video games).
- Meals where family members eat together and have conversation.
- Time spent alone with a parent or guardian.
- Occasions when the youth was welcomed to participate in making significant family decisions.
- Times the youth felt his or her opinion or desires didn't matter to the others in the household.

- Recreation or project activities done with parent(s) or family members.
- Conversations with family members about meaningful issues, concerns, and matters of faith.
- Time the family spent together helping others outside the family unit.
- Times when a family member's feelings were hurt or arguments occurred.

After the allotted time for completing the chart has expired, have the youth bring the information to a gathering of the group. Give each person an 11-by-17 sheet of paper and a pencil. Ask the youth to use the information from his or her chart to create a family graph that shows the "ups" and "downs" of time spent with the family. Discuss with the young people how the ups and downs made them feel.

Ask the youth to explore what each of them could do to improve the way their family interacts with one another. Have each youth write a letter to God that lists things he or she is prepared to do to create a better home life. Have the youth put their letters in envelopes, then address the envelopes to themselves. Collect all the sealed envelopes. (Mail the letters to the youth a few weeks later as a reminder of the promises they have made.) Close the time together with prayer, asking for God's guidance for each of the families represented in the group.

Bring It to the Sharing Basket

Send this activity home with youth as a way for families to start discussions, build mutual support, and grow together spiritually. Give the instructions verbally and also in writing so that the youth can take these home for their parent(s) to read. Ask the youth to find a container at home (or buy an inexpensive one) such as a basket, a decorative bowl, a finished wooden box, or a can that could be covered and decorated. This should be a container that can be dedicated permanently and exclusively for this purpose. The container needs an opening wide enough to put items in and take items out of easily. Make the container aesthetically pleasing so that it can be displayed in a prominent place in the home: a buffet, coffee table, kitchen table, or countertop. The intention is for it to be easily seen and readily used.

Plan a session during which all the youth bring the containers to the group meeting or retreat so that they can be dedicated for use by their family. The container provides a physical place for family members to drop meaningful ideas, stories, poems, prayers, Scripture passages, small items such as a pretty shell or rock, joys to celebrate, topics for family discussions, and so forth. Have the youth brainstorm about other types of items that might be placed in the container. The list of possibilities needs to be prepared and copied in time to be sent home with the containers, along with instructions for using the containers.

Instructions for Using the Sharing Basket

- Every family member collects and puts items (like those on the distributed list) in the basket or container.
- At a meal or before going to bed, have a family member pull one or more items out of the basket or container to read to the rest of the family. Enjoy and discuss the item(s), as appropriate.

This container offers a fun, ongoing way for the family to share items or thoughts deemed important by someone in the family. This practice opens up channels of communication, growth, and mutual understanding.

CHAPTER 13

ENCOUNTERS WITH GOD

First Glance

Before reading this chapter, reflect on this thought:
God said to Moses, "I AM WHO I AM." (Exodus 3:14a)

Heart to Heart

A burning bush caught Moses' attention. He walked over to check it out, and that was where God recruited him to lead a downtrodden people to freedom. God heard the cries of their travail under the oppressive regime of Pharaoh. A fascinating interplay ensued between God and Moses. Moses wanted to know God's name. He felt sure that the Israelites would quiz him about which god he claimed to represent. The Creator offered only this mysterious retort: "I AM WHO I AM." Then God said, "Thus you shall say to the Israelites, 'I AM has sent me to you'" (Exodus 3:14).

One might get the impression that God deliberately dodged Moses' question. This impression may be quite accurate. On the other hand, the reply returns so directly that few living in Moses' time would miss the intent. It all hinges on grasping the importance of a name in ancient times.

For the ancients, naming something or someone meant having a degree of power over the person or object. God had a message for Moses and the Israelites. We can paraphrase this message like this: "I will not be pigeonholed or limited by what you call me. I AM WHO I AM." God is so much more than any of us comprehend. The Life Behind All Life comes to us in countless expressions and will not be confined to notions that fit patterns with which we always feel comfortable. Despite the absurdity of such an endeavor, some folks display a need to corral the Source of the entire universe. They wish to give the impression that God can only be manifest in a way they designate. Usually, these sanctioned experiences of the Divine mirror the experience of the person advocating them. To be sure, God does come to such people in the fashion they affirm; yet it is presumptuous to suggest that God simply duplicates the same experience for everyone.

Many of us have a penchant for stalls. We want to, figuratively speaking, stand in one place like a horse, staring straight ahead. We expect God to appear to us in a mode we have determined as correct—to appear right in front of us, so to speak. And when this doesn't happen, we get disheartened and begin to wonder where God is. We miss the joy of getting out to exercise—that is, to exercise our capacity to see.

In reflecting on these paragraphs, we urge you to break free of the self-imposed boundaries that limit your experience of God. Leap the fences and roam unbridled through the vast territory of your life experiences. Remove the blinders that prevent you from taking in the sweeping panoramic view of God's presence with you over time and within the broad expanse of what's happening in the wider world. Look close by too, for the Holy One is right next to you in the midst of your everyday reality. *Emmanuel*—"God is with us"—dwells with us, but we sometimes don't have the eyes to see. A Bible study leader whom we know asks, half in jest and half serious: "Have you ever wondered how many burning bushes Moses walked by before he saw that one?" Good question.

Repeat the following prayer for approximately five minutes. Then pause several times during the day to repeat this prayer.

> Free me!
> Open my eyes to see you, God.
> Open my heart to feel you, God.
> Open my mind to hear you, God.

Ask yourself these questions: If a young person were to ask me, "Have you ever encountered God?" or "How do you know God is real?", what would I say? Which of my experiences would I characterize as experiences of God? Where and when have I sensed the presence of the Sacred?

 Real Life: Stories drawn from the lives of youth

| Note to Camp Counselor |

It may sound strange, but you introduced me to God. I've been told all my life that God is real, but I never felt God was really with me. You live your faith and inspire me to do the same. Your patience and gentleness warm my heart. It shows me that God is in you, and reminds me that God is in me too. I don't know how, but I know you love me. I thank God for you.

| Creek Watcher |

My family lives in the country. I love it out there. Because the nearest neighbor lives over a mile away, you can't see any other houses or even lights at night. I continually roam the hills, forests, and fields by myself, especially in the summer after finishing my chores. One of my favorite pastimes, when I'm in the right mood, is to find a spot in a forest or field and just sit. I find a comfortable niche, then try to blend in by being perfectly still. I remember starting this at about age eight.

It rarely bores me, because it seems so different each time. Some days I flip onto my back and watch the clouds roll by. At other times my mind starts to wander, and I lose all track of time. Occasionally I get so relaxed that I fall asleep outside. Amazing things happen too. Wild squirrels chasing each other have run right across my lap, even though it was the middle of hunting season. Early one fall, while leaning up against a tree, a deer came up from behind me and stuck her head right beside mine. I could actually hear her breathing. She pawed the ground nervously because she could smell me, but couldn't figure out where I was.

Creeks and rivers really draw me. I get down on my belly and creep up to the edge. Dragonflies mate inches from my eyes, and wary brook trout suck mayflies off the surface of the water, while I feel the warmth of the sun and smell the distinct odor of the various streams.

I don't know how to describe it exactly, but sometimes I feel this incredible oneness with the plants and the animals—well, with the universe, really. It sounds kind of silly when I say it out loud, but it's true. A peace, a gratitude, wells up inside me, and sometimes I even cry. I know that I am part of something way bigger than me. At these times, I often sense this Presence with me—not a person, though. I never see anyone. I feel this strong love around me, but no one is there. I don't talk with too many people about it, because I'm afraid they would think it's weird or think that I'm just psyching myself into it somehow. Once, I met another person who had similar experiences. She thought it was God. When I told my mom and dad, they agreed. I can't prove it, but in my heart I just somehow know it's God.

This Is Where You Belong

I just about quit youth ministry. Two o'clock in the morning was not a good hour to be out rounding up wayward teenagers on retreat who refused to stay in their cabins. I'd usher one group back to the appropriate place, then get word that others had slipped out while their counselor fell asleep. I don't know what came over the bunch of them. Sure, a few stragglers normally lingered a bit after lights out, but never had it gone on half the night with no end in sight. I felt so exhausted and so ignored in the futility of gaining the cooperation of a group who found great pleasure in not cooperating. I was genuinely worried about where they might have gone, with wilderness all around us, and what they might be doing.

Finally, in a secluded section of a trail, I sagged down on a stump and started crying. Working with the youth group was a major commitment, and I was already unsure whether or not to continue with it, considering all the other responsibilities in my life. This situation became the last straw. I sat there muttering to myself, "That's it. It's not worth it. Tomorrow morning we're packing up. This retreat is over! The time has come for me to bag volunteering for this." My mind was made up.

What happened next changed my life. A voice said very clearly, "This is where you belong." At first, I ignored it and continued my stifled tirade. Again, a distinct voice strongly reiterated the very same words: "This is where you belong." It didn't come from the sky or anything. It spoke within my own mind, somehow; but it wasn't my voice, nor was I making it up. I remember replying out loud, "Leave me alone." I didn't want to hear this, because I had made my final decision. Again the voice: "This is where you belong." Finally, I got the point and resigned myself to praying for guidance to resolve this situation.

The next day during a heart-to-heart talk with the teenagers about the incidents of the night before, the right words just came to me. The words instantly transformed the attitudes of the youth, and the remainder of the event was a powerful experience of Christian community. Nothing quite like this had ever happened to me before, nor since. How do I interpret this incident? God spoke to me—that's my only explanation. I know it certainly does not happen to everyone, and it doesn't have to. God comes to us in so many ways. In this case, God literally spoke to me at a time when I needed it, and for nearly twenty-five years I have continued to serve as an adult worker with youth. Looking back, I wouldn't trade this experience for the world.

Questions: In what ways did these people encounter God? What would it mean for youth who are seeking God to hear others talk about the different ways they experience God? How do these modern-day occurrences continue God's movement as recorded in the Bible?

Delving Deeper

As a deer longs for flowing streams,
    so my soul longs for you, O God.
My soul thirsts for God,
    for the living God.
When shall I come and behold
    the face of God?
          (Psalm 42:1-2)

Like most of us, youth eventually want to do more than simply talk about God. Young people long to experience the Creator. When they do and recognize God for themselves, it produces a "twist of faith" like no other.

Spiritual leaders face a dilemma, though. God is invisible; the mysterious nature of I AM defies our senses. We may be created in the image of God, but that doesn't mean that God is a giant human being! How do we introduce youth to a God who cannot be seen or even touched in the way that we commonly understand these terms and sensations?

Youth today communicate visually more and more. They learn through rapid-fire pictures, like those on MTV and on shows geared specifically toward teenagers. So don't be surprised when youth present you with the challenge: "If God is real, prove it. Show us God." After all, for many teenagers, *seeing* represents their primary mode of knowing the world about them. The challenge before adult leaders is to teach youth new ways of sensing—to encourage them to develop eyes and hearts that can recognize and relate to the energy and presence of the Divine.

God comes to us humans all the time. Some recognize God; others don't. There are at least four things adult leaders can do to support the life of faith of youth. First, engage the youth in truly seeking God with the assurance that if they don't find God, God will find them. Second, expose them to past and present examples of people who have encountered God and how these individuals have experienced that encounter. Third, be consistently clear that the young person's experience with God does not need to match anyone else's experience. God comes in different ways to different people. Fourth, offer the youth some clues about how to evaluate whether or not an experience is an experience of God.

Encounters With God: Examples of How People Experience God's Presence

Below are examples taken from Scripture and from the Wesleyan heritage of ways in which a variety of people have experienced God's presence in their lives. Use these examples to help the youth reflect on different ways in which God interacts with them and with others.

- *Encountering God in Jesus*

   From his fullness we have all received, grace upon grace. The law indeed was given through Moses; grace and truth came through Jesus Christ. No one has ever seen God. It is God the only Son, who is close to the Father's heart, who has made him known.   (John 1:16-18)

   A week later his disciples were again in the house, and Thomas was with them. Although the doors were shut, Jesus came and stood among them and said, "Peace be with you." Then he said to Thomas, "Put your finger here and see my hands. Reach out your hand and put it in my side. Do not doubt but believe." Thomas answered him, "My Lord and my God!" Jesus said to him, "Have you believed because you have seen me? Blessed are those who have not seen and yet have come to believe." (John 20:26-29)

- *Experiencing God through nature*

    For what can be known about God is plain to them, because God has shown it to them. Ever since the creation of the world [God's] eternal power and divine nature, invisible though they are, have been understood and seen through the things [God] has made. So they are without excuse; for though they knew God, they did not honor him as God or give thanks to him, but they became futile in their thinking, and their senseless minds were darkened. Claiming to be wise, they became fools; and they exchanged the glory of the immortal God for images resembling a mortal human being or birds or four-footed animals or reptiles. (Romans 1:19-21)

- *Experiencing God in loving relationships*

    Beloved, let us love one another, because love is from God; everyone who loves is born of God and knows God. Whoever does not love does not know God, for God is love. (1 John 4:7-8)

- *Experiencing God in doing good and avoiding evil (harm)*

    Beloved, do not imitate what is evil but imitate what is good. Whoever does good is from God; whoever does evil has not seen God. (3 John 1:11)

- *Experiencing God by seeking God with the whole heart through spiritual disciplines and practices*

    The spiritual disciplines include prayer, searching the Scriptures, celebrating the Lord's Supper, fasting, participating in Christian conversation, doing no harm and doing good, attending worship, meditating and practicing the presence of God, going on retreats in nature, and maintaining a spiritual journal and writing letters. (See Chapter 4, "Lead On!", for a discussion of the spiritual disciplines.) One illustration of experiencing God's presence while practicing a spiritual discipline comes from the life of John Wesley. While attending a society meeting in Aldersgate Street in London in 1738, Wesley had a defining experience with God in which he felt God touch his heart in a powerful way. He later wrote about the experience in his journal: ". . . I felt my heart strangely warmed. I felt I did trust in Christ, Christ alone for salvation: And an assurance was given me, that He had taken away *my* sins, even *mine*, and saved *me* from the law of sin and death."[1]

1 "Journal from October 14, 1735, to November 29, 1745," in The *Works of John Wesley Volume I* (Zondervan Publishing House, n.d.); p. 103.

- *Experiencing God through dreams and visions*

  Her husband Joseph, being a righteous man and unwilling to expose her to public disgrace, planned to dismiss her quietly. But just when he had resolved to do this, an angel of the Lord appeared to him in a dream and said, "Joseph, son of David, do not be afraid to take Mary as your wife, for the child conceived in her is from the Holy Spirit. She will bear a son, and you are to name him Jesus, for he will save his people from their sins."   (Matthew 1:19-21)

- *Experiencing God through angels and voices*

  In that region there were shepherds living in the fields, keeping watch over their flock by night. Then an angel of the Lord stood before them, and the glory of the Lord shone around them, and they were terrified. But the angel said to them, "Do not be afraid; for see—I am bringing you good news of great joy for all the people: to you is born this day in the city of David a Savior, who is the Messiah, the Lord. This will be a sign for you: you will find a child wrapped in bands of cloth and lying in a manger."   (Luke 2:8-12)

  - *Experiencing God in miracles and other wonders*

    Now there was a Pharisee named Nicodemus, a leader of the Jews. He came to Jesus by night and said to him, "Rabbi, we know that you are a teacher who has come from God; for no one can do these signs that you do apart from the presence of God."   (John 3:1-2)

- *Experiencing God through acts of repentance and reconciliation*

  Jacob said, "No, please; if I find favor with you [his brother Esau], then accept my present from my hand; for truly to see your face is like seeing the face of God—since you have received me with such favor."   (Genesis 33:10)

- *Experiencing God through gatherings of people of faith*

  For where two or three are gathered in my name, I am there among them.   (Matthew 18:20)

- *Experiencing God in struggles for justice*

  All Israel heard of the judgment that the king had rendered; and they stood in awe of the king, because they perceived that the wisdom of God was in him, to execute justice.   (1 Kings 3:28)

  The LORD works vindication
      and justice for all who are oppressed.
  He made known his ways to Moses,
      his acts to the people of Israel.

The LORD is merciful and gracious,
    slow to anger and abounding in steadfast love.
                      (Psalm 103:6-8)

Evaluating an Experience

How do we discern whether or not a particular experience is an experience of God? At the risk of being simplistic, we offer these questions as a way to assess the genuineness of a religious experience:

1. Does this experience lead me to do justice, love kindness, and walk humbly with God? (Micah 6:8).
2. Does this experience produce the fruit of the Spirit? When we connect with God's Spirit, it moves us to be more loving, joyful, peaceful, patient, kind, generous, faithful (trustworthy and full of faith), gentle, and self-controlled (Galatians 5:22-23).
3. Does this experience draw me into unity and mutual concern with other people seeking God (Ephesians 4:1-7)?

As a spiritual leader with youth, where do you start your efforts to lead teenagers toward encounters with God—or better, toward recognizing God's presence that is already with them? The following assessment by a thirteen-year-old of how she began to recognize God offers some hints for answering this question: "I feel this connection with a group of people. They love me and accept me, even if they just met me. I experience God in the way they treat me, as we get to know each other better. It happens less in a big worship service where there are hundreds of people; I think it's because I don't really know a lot of those people well. Almost every time I feel God, though, we are focusing on God or on being with God on purpose. I almost never do this in other places, like at school. Maybe that's why I have fun at school, but rarely feel close to God there."

 Tuning In: Ways to know how youth encounter God

Below are a few activities a leader can use to tune into the variety of ways in which youth encounter God's presence.

- *Prepare a sermon:* Have youth describe their own relationship with God using the statements below. Ask the youth to complete each of the statements at three different times, writing a different response for each statement each time—provided that all the responses are true to their experience. Ask two youth who feel comfortable speaking in public to gather the anonymous responses and to work with the pastor to prepare a sermon entitled "Experiencing God Today." (If you are working with only one youth, use the questions below as a survey. Have the young person ask the same questions of adults whom the youth like, either in the congregation or in other settings. This information can still be used by the pastor and the youth to help create a sermon.) Use the sermon on "Youth Sunday" when the youth lead worship.

"I feel closest to God when . . ."

"God helps people by . . ."

"I would say that my most meaningful experiences with God are . . ."

"If I wanted to connect more with God, I would . . ."

"I see God moving in the world through . . ."

- *Create a real-life video:* Using a video camera, have the teenagers record church leaders and/or teachers while at church or in a camp setting. Have these adults tell about an important experience in their lives when they felt God's presence or guidance. Have the youth watch these recordings and discuss what they learned.
- *Find reassurance:* Have the youth read the following passages and circle the words or phrases that remind them of God's presence with them. Then ask them to share times when they felt God's presence or when they found it difficult to believe or to remember God's presence. Close in prayer.

Then when you call upon me and come and pray to me, I will hear you. When you search for me, you will find me; if you seek me with all your heart.

(Jeremiah 29:12-13)

Where can I go from your spirit?
    Or where can I flee from your presence?
If I ascend to heaven, you are there;
    if I make my bed in Sheol, you are there.
If I take the wings of the morning
    and settle at the farthest limits of the sea,
even there your hand shall lead me,
    and your right hand shall hold me fast.

(Psalm 139:7-10)

And remember, I am with you always, to the end of the age.   (Matthew 28:20b)

Which one of you, having a hundred sheep and losing one of them, does not leave the ninety-nine in the wilderness and go after the one that is lost until he finds it? When he has found it, he lays it on his shoulders and rejoices. And when he comes home, he calls together his friends and neighbors, saying to them, "Rejoice with me, for I have found my sheep that was lost."   (Luke 15:4-6)

Twists of Faith: Activities that make a faith connection

Use the following activities to help youth connect their faith with the experiences of God's presence they have in their everyday lives.

Start a Spiritual Discipline

Over time, introduce spiritual practices as pathways to connecting with God. (See Chapter 4, "Lead On!", for more information on the spiritual disciplines). During a meeting with the youth, provide an overview of the spiritual disciplines. Then ask the youth to take time to practice the disciplines in their own lives. After sufficient time (perhaps one or two weeks), ask each youth to choose one or two disciplines that he or she would like to practice on an ongoing basis. Connect the youth with resources such as *Devo'Zine* magazine, accountability groups, and so forth. Do not put them on guilt trips! Remember, the focus of practicing the spiritual disciplines is on growing closer to God. If you have a group or camp setting, incorporate a few specific spiritual practices into the group life on a regular basis.

Hear a Word From God

Take the youth to a quiet natural setting. Each will need a pad of paper and a pencil. Give the youth the following instructions, both verbally and in writing. Answer any questions they may have before they get started.

1. Find a place where you can be undisturbed, yet close enough to other members of the group to be seen and heard, should you call. You will be in this place for thirty minutes.
2. Get comfortable so you can be very still and blend in with your surroundings. Remaining as silent as possible, start scanning the natural world around you, trying to notice everything. Begin with the point farthest away and then move your eyes closer and closer until you are looking at the surroundings right around where you're sitting.
3. Choose one plant, animal, insect, rock, or other item from nature to get to know in great detail. Using your pad and paper, write down every characteristic of this object that you can see. Look very closely. (You may even need a magnifying glass.) Touch and smell the object, if possible. Does the object or animal make a sound? Write down thoughts and detailed observations about the experience. How does the experience with the object or animal make you feel inside? What emotions do you feel? How is your animal or object connected with or affected by its surroundings? What does it contribute to the well-being of other creatures?
4. Give the object or animal you have observed a name that expresses some characteristic or feeling about it you've noticed. Meister Eckhart, a person of faith who particularly loved God's world, once said: "All creatures are words of God."[2] What does this creature or object from

2 *Breakthrough: Meister Eckhart's Creation Spirituality in New Translation.* Introduction and Commentaries by Matthew Fox, O.P. (Image Books, 1980); p. 58.

the community of God's creation say to you about life? What might God be trying to say to you through this creature or object? Or to turn the focus around: Since God created it, what might this animal or object be saying about who God is and what God is like? Jot down all your responses to these questions.

5. When you have finished with your meditation, quietly return to the group leader or continue to enjoy the place you have selected until you see everyone returning.

When all the youth have returned, divide them into pairs. Ask each pair to talk about the creature or object each person has selected and what he or she named it. Have persons in the pairs tell each other what they think God might be saying to them about life through the creature or object they have discovered. Finally, ask members of the pairs to share with each other what the animal or object might be saying about what God is like. After sufficient time, gather the whole group and have them form a prayer circle. Ask those who are willing to pray, mentioning things about nature and God for which they are thankful.

The list below contains some of the most helpful resources we found related to the subject matter of this book.

The Bottom Line: How to Help Youth Become Disciples, by Greg McKinnon (Abingdon Press, 1998).

Capture the Moment: Building Faith Traditions for Families, by Rick and Sue Isbell (Discipleship Resources, 1998).

Caring From the Inside Out: How to Help Youth Show Compassion, by Soozung Sa (Abingdon Press, 1997).

The Choice Is Yours: A Teenager's Guide to Self-Discovery, Relationships, Values, and Spiritual Growth, by Bonnie M. Parsley and Scott Peck (Fireside, 1992).

Faith for Tough Times, by David Cassady (Group Publishing Inc., 1991).

The Godbearing Life: The Art of Soul-Tending for Youth Ministry, by Kenda Creasy Dean, Ron Foster, and Rita Collett (The Upper Room, 1998).

Go For It: 25 Faith-Building Adventures for Groups, by Walt Marcum (Abingdon Press, 1998).

Helping Youth Pray: How to Connect Youth With God, by Greg McKinnon (Abingdon Press, 1997).

Man's Search for Meaning, by Viktor E. Frankl (Buccaneer Books, 1993).

The Ministry of Nurture: How to Build Real-Life Faith Into Your Kids, by Duffy Robbins (Zondervan Publishing House, 1990).

On Death and Dying, by Elisabeth Kubler-Ross (Collier Books, 1997).

Postmoderns: The Beliefs, Hopes, & Fears of Young Americans (1965-1981), by Craig Kennet Miller (Discipleship Resources, 1996).

Raising Self-Reliant Children in a Self-Indulgent World: Seven Building Blocks for Developing Capable Young People, by H. Stephen Glenn and Jane Nelsen, Ed.D. (Prima Publishing, 1989).

The Seven Habits of Highly Effective People, by Stephen R. Covey (Simon & Schuster, 1989).

The Shelter of Each Other: Rebuilding Our Families, by Mary Pipher, Ph.D. (Ballantine Books, 1997).

SkillAbilities for Youth Ministry, a series published 1997 and 1998 (Abingdon Press).

Songs, compiled by Yohann Anderson (Songs and Creations, Inc., 1972, 1992).

The Youth Worker's Handbook to Family Ministry: Strategies and Practical Ideas for Reaching Your Students' Families, by Chap Clark (Zondervan Publishing House, 1997).

The Bible and Faith

All About Jesus

Back-to-the-Bible Basics

Being a Faithful Disciple

The Christmas Story

Creation and Creating

Do Miracles Really Happen?

Elements of Worship

Freedom: What Is It, and Where Do I Get It?

Fruit of the Spirit

Getting Closer to God

God's Forgiveness

The Grace of God: What Is It?

Hope for the Future

I Have Doubts and Questions

Lent: What and Why?

The Lord's Prayer—Paraphrased

The Music of Life

Other Religions

The Parables

Prayer and Meditation

Resurrection

Sacraments: What Do They Mean?

Symbols of Our Faith

Temptation

Unsolved Mysteries of the Bible

What Does Holy Communion Mean?

What Is Faith?

What Is Pentecost?

Where Do We See God?

Who Is God?

Who Is the Holy Spirit?

Individual Issues and Faith

Accepting Myself and Others

Being in Leadership

Being Shy Can Be Tough

Dealing With Stress

Decision-Making—What to Do?

Eating Disorders—Who Can Help?

Feeling Angry: Finding Positive Solutions

Getting Organized

How Can I Overcome Fear?

I'm So Bored!

In Search of Meaning in My Life

I Worry About . . .

Leaving Home After Graduation

Learning to Really Listen

Living for Better Health and Fun

Making My Own Space

Materialism—I Want . . .

My Bedroom

My Unique Gifts From God

Preparing for Adulthood

Setting Goals and Dreams

Sticky Situations: Do I Cop Out or Do I Cope?

Suicide: Feelings, Signs, Resources

Taking Responsibility for My Actions

Taking Risks

What if I Fail?

What? Me a Minister?

What's My Self-Image?

When I Feel Like Giving Up

When I'm Lonely

Why Do I Do What I Do? Values and Behaviors

Relationships and Faith

Conflict Resolution

Dating: What's It All About?

Deepening Relationships

Facing My Mistakes

Forgiveness, Comfort,
    Encouragement

Gift Giving

Gossip: Taming the Tongue

In All Honesty . . .

Loving Those We Don't Even Like

My Family's a Mess

People I Admire and Why

Saying Thank You

Sensuality, Sexuality, and Faith

Stereotypes and Labeling

Those Weird Things Parents Do

The Walls I Build

What Does God Want Me to Do?

What if Mom or Dad Dies?

What Is This Thing Called Love?

You Are Not Alone

Social Issues and Faith

Advertising Messages

AIDS—Important Questions

Bumper-Sticker Hunt

Christians and Drinking

Diversity: Appreciating Our
    Differences

Following the Rules

Healthy Competition

Homelessness

Hunger: Can I Make a Difference?

Other Cultures: Lifestyles, Music,
    and More

Poverty and Missions

Taking Care of God's Creation

Teen Parenting

United Methodist Social Principles

War

What's News? The Media

When Should I Speak Out?